Teaching with Hacker Handbooks

Topics, Strategies, and Lesson Plans

Marcy Carbajal Van Horn

St. Edward's University

With contributions from

Elizabeth Canfield

Virginia Commonwealth University

Nancy Sommers

Harvard University

Terry Myers Zawacki

George Mason University

Bedford / St. Martin's

Boston ◆ New York

Manufactured in the United States of America.

6 5 4 3 2 1
f e d c b a

For information, write: Bedford/St. Martin's, 75 Arlington Street, Boston, MA 02116 (617-399-4000)

ISBN: 978-1-4576-1918-2

Foreword

Dear Colleagues:

As the lead author of the current editions of Hacker handbooks, I have traveled around the United States, talking with students and teachers at colleges and universities, inside and outside of classrooms. It is a joy to watch instructors in action and to meet so many dedicated teachers, both novice and veteran, who develop innovative ways to integrate Hacker handbooks into their courses. At every school I visit, questions arise regarding the best practices for teaching academic writing, effective approaches for meeting the needs of today's students, and time-saving methods for reading and responding to student writing. Teachers seek practical solutions to real classroom challenges and are eager to learn from one another.

Teaching with Hacker Handbooks, written by Marcy Carbajal Van Horn, with contributions from experienced teachers of academic writing, provides a wealth of innovative and imaginative ideas for integrating the lessons of Hacker handbooks into your classroom. We've chosen these lessons in response to specific classroom needs. In my visit to Missouri State University, for instance, a group of teachers discussed the challenges of helping students learn to write and revise clear and engaging thesis statements. At Palm Beach and Green River Community Colleges, I joined similar conversations about teaching students to pose authentic questions that would lead to thoughtful arguments. And at Wright State University and the University of Connecticut, teachers asked for resources to help students learn to summarize, paraphrase, quote from, and integrate sources—key skills for academic writing. In all these conversations, I've been struck by the teachers' desire to unite the lessons of the handbook with the lessons of the classroom. Many wanted to make sure that their handbook becomes a used and useful reference, a companion both in the composition course and during a student's entire college writing career.

Teaching is a collaborative enterprise, and we've designed *Teaching with Hacker Handbooks* so that instructors can learn from their fellow practitioners. I would certainly have benefited from such a resource during my first year teaching composition, when I was a work-in-progress, learning each lesson along with my students, sometimes (but not always) one step ahead. And I know that the wisdom and practical knowledge this collection offers will appeal to both novice and veteran teachers looking to put Hacker handbooks to work in their classrooms. As with all new projects, this resource is also a work-in-progress. It will continue to grow as you and your colleagues provide feedback and new ideas, and I hope that it will inspire you to contribute to the teaching conversation we have started here.

—Nancy Sommers

Introduction to *Teaching with Hacker Handbooks*

Welcome to *Teaching with Hacker Handbooks*. My goal in creating this resource was to support both new and seasoned composition instructors who are striving to help their students get the most out of their handbook and their course. With contributions from teachers across the United States, including discussions authored by Nancy Sommers (Harvard University), Terry Myers Zawacki (George Mason University), and Elizabeth Canfield (Virginia Commonwealth University), and timely advice from our editorial review board (Linda DiDesidero, University of Maryland; Laura Detmering, formerly of Northern Kentucky University, now at the University of Louisville; Kathy Keating, Greensboro College; and Tony Procell, El Paso Community College), this collection provides that support. The creators of these resources acknowledge that many new instructors need straightforward advice for building a writing course from the ground up. We also recognize that even experienced instructors welcome the sharing of fresh ideas and reminders of proven practices.

Teaching with Hacker Handbooks includes advice on planning an effective course, strategies for tying the handbook to assignments and class activities, and an extensive collection of samples from college instructors in various teaching situations across the country. These resources will help you and your students get the most out of class time and class materials while building critical skills for college-level writing in composition and beyond.

Features

Best practices for improving your course.   Part I of *Teaching with Hacker Handbooks* offers proven advice for building or enhancing your own composition or writing-intensive course. Developed with input from a community of seasoned instructors, the topics in Part I provide class-tested methods and models that will engage students in their own learning:

- Planning a course and designing a syllabus
- Designing effective assignments
- Responding to student writing
- Working with multilingual writers (Teaching ESL)
- Addressing writing in the disciplines

These topics contain cross-references to the lesson modules in Part II.

Practical strategies for common classroom goals. Part II presents lesson modules covering essential topics in writing instruction — such as teaching thesis statements, helping students avoid plagiarism, and developing visual literacy. Packed with advice and practices from the composition community, each module is presented in a stepped-out, three-part format that will help you make the most of your time:

- The Challenges section briefly introduces some of the teaching and learning challenges you and your students may encounter when you cover the topic in class.

- The Strategies portion of the module describes techniques and activities you can use to address the challenges in various situations. It also includes a step-by-step sample lesson that thoroughly illustrates — with models, prompts, and handouts — how to carry out one or more of the suggested activities in class.

- The Resources grid at the end of each module directs you to the sections, exercises, and ancillaries from all of the Hacker handbooks that reinforce the lesson. You can quickly scan the grid to find the sections and pages that will best serve you and your students.

Together, the modules offer effective practices that will help your students learn the value of their handbooks as a reference for the classroom or online learning environment and for working on their own.

Model syllabi and assignments, ready to tailor. Part III of *Teaching with Hacker Handbooks* includes a sampling of syllabi and assignments to which you can refer as you build your own course. These selections, which present a variety of course types and teaching approaches, show how other instructors have integrated the handbooks into their teaching. With contributions from a community of writing instructors in programs across the country, this collection of authentic materials can inspire you with fresh ideas, whether you are a new or veteran composition instructor.

For electronic versions of the materials in this book, and for new contributions to these resources, you can visit hackerhandbooks.com/teaching. For additional resources, visit the instructor side of your handbook's companion Web site:

The Bedford Handbook: hackerhandbooks.com/bedhandbook

A Writer's Reference: hackerhandbooks.com/writersref

Rules for Writers: hackerhandbooks.com/rules

A Pocket Style Manual: hackerhandbooks.com/pocket

— Marcy Carbajal Van Horn

Contents

Topics

Part I presents topics you might consider prior to starting your course.

Notes

Topic 1
Designing and planning your writing course

Before you begin teaching the course, you must establish a plan. The advice in this topic can help you design an effectively sequenced schedule for a process-based writing course.

Mapping out a writing course

Each instructor has a different method for establishing a course schedule. Some instructors like to work organically, assigning projects inspired by current events or the students' own experiences. Other instructors approach their tasks systematically, planning assignments for the entire semester before the first day of class. If you're just starting your career as an instructor, a thorough plan might work best. This topic offers tips for adopting a systematic approach.

Begin by identifying your course outcomes.   Find out what your department expects your course to accomplish by asking questions such as the following:

- When students exit a course at this level, what skills are they expected to have acquired?

- Does this class require specific types of assignments, such as in-class timed writing or long-term research papers?

- How does your course serve the school? Is it a prerequisite for other courses?

Your department liaison should be able to provide this information for you. If the department isn't able to furnish you with official course outcomes, you can find the information you need by reviewing the syllabi of other instructors.

Learn about your context.   Once you've identified the course outcomes, learn as much as possible about your student population. Even though you will not have met your students at this stage in the planning process, you can anticipate trends and patterns by asking your department chair or other instructors, or by performing a quick search on your school's Web site. (Many school Web sites include pages that list student statistics.) Knowing this information will help you tailor your assignments

Questions to ask about students in your context

Experience

- Will your classes be filled with traditionally aged college students, who likely have some prior knowledge of traditional rhetorical essay forms (such as the five-paragraph model), argumentation strategies, and citation conventions?
- Will you have any nontraditional students who are returning to school after years in the workforce or at home?
- Do many students in your context typically come from high schools that don't require much writing?
- Are many of your students coming out of developmental courses that might require no more than paragraph-length writing?
- Have all the students in your class followed your school's typical writing course sequence, or have some taken other writing-intensive courses outside of your department?
- Are any honors students enrolled in your course?

Goals

- What are your students' majors?
- Are all the students following the same degree track (AS, AA, BS, BA, and so on)?
- In general, how many writing-intensive courses will students take after they complete your course?

Workload, time management, and special considerations

- What is your ratio of part-time to full-time students?
- Do students in your context typically have part-time or full-time responsibilities (either in or outside the home) in addition to their college work? How are these commitments likely to affect their participation in your course?
- Will you have student athletes who may miss classes for games or other events? If so, what is your school's policy for accommodating athletes?
- Will you have a large number of multilingual writers who will need help with language development as well as writing skills? What additional services (tutors or writing labs, for example) does your school provide for such students?
- Are any students registered with the disabilities service office at your school? If so, what accommodations will they require?

to meet your students' general needs and build in enough steps to scaffold your assignments effectively.

Determine the number and types of assignments you'll require.   Many process-based writing courses for first- and second-year students build in four to six major writing assignments per semester, sometimes with additional informal writing tasks. The number and types of assignments you can offer will depend heavily on the background knowledge and prior experience of your students. The less experienced your students are, the more steps you will likely have to build into each assignment. If you expect that you will have to accommodate a wide range of skill levels, consider planning a few challenging assignment variations for more advanced students.

If you will be serving a nontraditional or other specific population (for instance, second-career students, student athletes, multilingual writers, developmental writers, or students with disabilities), try to include assignments that accommodate their needs and guide them toward achieving the course goals. Better yet, think about assignments that might draw on their particular talents and experiences.

If you're uncertain about the types of assignments to require, ask your department chair or other instructors for samples.

Establish benchmarks for achievement.   Consider creating a rubric, a grid that matches essay features with descriptions of various levels of achievement, to establish benchmarks for your course. More simply, describe in detail the standard features of an A or excellent paper, a B or above-average paper, and so on. Include specific descriptions of the features you plan to assess, such as development, organization, expression and style, and sentence-level control. If discussion and peer review will contribute to the grade, clarify those expectations as well.

For a sample rubric and additional discussion, see "Work with rubrics" in Topic 3, "Responding to student writing."

Although not all papers will fit neatly into these grade categories, the rubric can provide a general structure that will help both you and your students. If you choose, you can attach the rubric to your syllabus so that students are aware of your grading standards from the beginning of the course, and you can use assignment-specific versions of this rubric when you assess student work.

Set due dates at regular intervals over the semester.   After you have determined the number of assignments, rough out the due dates by dividing the number of weeks in the semester by the number of assignments you plan to give. For example, in a fifteen-week course with five major assignments, you can plan to devote approximately three weeks to each assignment, making adjustments for shorter or more demanding tasks as necessary. Distributing major assignments throughout the course benefits students and instructors. Students will have sufficient time for planning, drafting, and revising, and you will have enough time to evaluate papers and offer feedback before the next major assignment is due.

Build in enough time for writing, review, and revision.   When planning the course, begin with a simple timeline that maps the number of class periods you'll have with your students and the number of assignments you'll give. For each assignment, reserve a minimum of three class sessions for planning and review:

- At least one class session for explaining the assignment and previewing models
- At least one session for reviewing preliminary drafts (sometimes, scheduling two or more days is preferable). This review period allows for both peer feedback and your feedback on the draft.

- One session (or a partial session), at the time papers are returned or shortly after, for students to ask questions about your comments and begin to apply your feedback

If possible, consider adding days for students to plan or draft the essay in class, perform self-assessments, review citation conventions, and conduct research. In addition, give yourself sufficient time to grade and return assignments before students begin the next paper. (One week is typically a realistic target for a class of twenty-five to thirty-five students.) Sprinkle in additional skill-building activities on other days: preparing for assignments with reading and discussion, reviewing sentence-level issues and working on exercises, and generating ideas with in-class or informal writing assignments.

Here's a sample assignment schedule for a class that meets three times a week:

	Monday	Wednesday	Friday
Week 1	Discuss a reading to prepare for an assignment.	Introduce the assignment and preview model essays.	**Outline due.** Discuss organization and content, perhaps as a peer review session.
Week 2	Hand back the previous assignment, and review feedback in class.	**Draft 1 due.** Lead students through a self-assessment, checking for purpose and the use of sources (or other assignment requirement).	Revision workshop: Discuss model introductions and conclusions from the handbook.
Week 3	**Draft 2 due.** Conduct a peer review workshop.	Editing workshop: Review a sentence-level topic from the handbook (such as commas) and discuss editing strategies.	**Final draft due.** Write a cover letter in class.

Determining assignment sequences

When you design assignments for your course, create opportunities for students to build on skills they have previously practiced. Begin with an assignment that requires the fewest new skills. Then, with each subsequent assignment, increase the challenge by requiring the use of one or two new skills that you've covered in class.

Sample assignment sequence for a beginning-level writing course

Assignment 1: Basic essay   Focus on three basic features: purpose (thesis statement), organization (topic sentences and appropriate transitions), and development (coherent paragraphs with the use of concrete details).

Assignment 2: Summary or simple analysis of one text   Focus on quoting, paraphrasing, and using signal phrases, along with basics from Assignment 1.

Assignment 3: Analysis essay in MLA style (one text)   Focus on critical thinking (inference) and MLA style.

Assignment 4: Analysis essay in MLA style (two texts)   Require two texts so that students learn to refer to more than one author and practice synthesizing sources; focus on analytical (evaluative) thinking.

Assignment 5: Research paper in MLA style (multiple sources)   Require research and the evaluation of sources, more sophisticated signal phrases, and more complex citations in the works cited list.

In a first-semester writing course, for example, you could begin with a relatively simple essay assignment that focuses on the basics of purpose (crafting a thesis), organization (planning topic sentences), and development (writing effective paragraphs). The next essay might require students to add one new focus to the previous three: the integration of one source. The third essay could build on the first two assignments by requiring the use of two sources cited in MLA style. Continue scaffolding the assignments in manageable steps. See the sample assignment sequence for a beginning-level writing course.

Striking a balance between global and local issues

Novice writers typically need help with learning to analyze texts, construct arguments, structure their thoughts, and develop an academic voice. Often they also need help with recognizing sentence-level errors in their own work and using resources (such as the handbook) to find answers to their questions. Finding the time to address these needs in class is challenging, and you may struggle to balance your coverage of global issues (such as critical thinking, analysis, and research) with local issues (such as paragraphing and punctuation).

To ensure that students devote enough attention to both global and local writing issues, build a series of "workshop" days into the course calendar. For each writing assignment, schedule at least one workshop during the drafting stage to address global issues and at least one workshop during the revision stage to address local issues. Let the needs of your students and the demands of the assignment determine the topics you cover in each workshop. Ask students to prepare for these workshop sessions by bringing drafts of their papers. Structure each session so that students have time to write, review, or otherwise engage with their own work in class.

Conduct a workshop on global issues during the drafting stage. Early in the writing process, conduct at least one workshop in which students consider global strategies. For instance, if your students are working on an essay with an argumentative purpose, you can begin the workshop by discussing the argumentation strategies outlined in the handbook or reader. Review any sample thesis statements or outlines that the handbook or reader provides, and ask students to compare their work to the models. Give the students an opportunity to share their ideas and receive feedback, either from the whole class or from a few peers.

Conduct a workshop on local issues during the revision stage. Later in the writing process, after students have drafted their papers, guide them through one or more revision and editing workshops focused on local issues. For example, you might begin an editing workshop by discussing the sections in the handbook that cover comma usage. Review a few flawed sentences (either from the handbook exercises or from students' own papers) and work together to correct them by applying tips from the handbook. Then give students an opportunity to check their own work for similar errors and to receive feedback from you or from a few peers. See the sample workshop series for additional ideas.

Sample workshop series for an argument essay assignment

Day 1 (global issues) Discuss a few argument and persuasion readings; assign a position paper on a related topic. Have students brainstorm possible positions or topics with their peers.

Day 2 (global issues) Students bring rough outlines to class. Review model thesis statements from the handbook and lead students through a peer review of their rough outlines. Have students discuss whether their own thesis statements are debatable. Encourage them to revise their thesis statements, seeking feedback from you or from peers as necessary.

Day 3 (global issues) Students bring skeletal drafts or developed outlines to class. Review the content and organization of a few model outlines or papers. Discuss ethical, emotional, and logical appeals, and look for examples of these appeals in the models. Ask students to exchange their work with a few peers to evaluate the quality of their own appeals. Encourage them to revise the content of their outlines in class.

Day 4 (local issues) Students bring complete drafts to class. Discuss the sections in the handbook that cover coherent paragraphs and cohesive elements (transitions). Ask students to revise for coherence in class, exchanging papers with peers for additional feedback. (Students having trouble with coherence may find that they need to return to global revision and reconsider the overall structure of their essays.)

→

Day 5 (local issues) Students bring revised drafts to class. Discuss the handbook section on run-on sentences, and answer any questions students may have about the practice exercises. Ask students to exchange papers to identify run-on sentences in their peers' work. Once students have identified errors, have them return papers to the owners for editing.

Day 6 (local issues) Students bring final drafts to class. Discuss the section on commas from the handbook, and review a few of the practice exercises. Ask students to do last-minute editing for commas before they submit their papers for grading.

Integrating the handbook

Your handbook is much more than just a grammar reference book or citation tool. You can weave selections from the handbook into your course schedule at all stages of the writing process, from planning and composing to researching and evaluating sources to revising paragraphs and editing sentences. Scan the table of contents for topics that you will be covering, and assign sections as background reading for class discussions. Review the sample paragraphs and model essays in class to introduce or reinforce specific formatting and rhetorical advice. If necessary, assign the practice exercises for some topics (such as thesis statements and citations) to the whole class and reserve exercises on other topics (such as apostrophes and parallelism) for individual students with particular trouble spots.

The more students use the handbook under your guidance, the more comfortable they will become with using it on their own. If possible, take time to show students how to navigate the text to find specific advice. Doing so will help them understand why they have been asked to purchase the book and how the book can help them beyond a single assignment or the composition course. Consider using a scavenger hunt as a pairs activity that asks students to locate specific content in the handbook.

See hackerhandbooks.com/ teaching for a sample scavenger hunt.

Designing a syllabus

The syllabus is the contract between you and your students, and as such it should include information that supports both you and them. Many schools have specific guidelines for the design or structure of a syllabus. Ask your department chair or liaison to provide you with a model before you write yours. If your school does not have specific guidelines, include at least the following details: your contact information, the course description and outcomes, required textbooks, and key policies (see the box "Sections of a syllabus" for details). Add any other information you think will be valuable to you and your students.

Turn to the back of this collection and visit hackerhandbooks.com/ teaching for a variety of sample syllabi.

Sections of a syllabus

Critical components

- Course information: number, section, meeting times, dates, location
- Instructor contact information: name, office location, phone number, e-mail address, office hours
- Textbooks: titles, authors, where to purchase
- Grading policy: distribution of assignments, grade scale
- Attendance policy
- Late and makeup work policy
- Academic integrity or plagiarism policy
- Class schedule: a list of readings and assignments or directions for finding the class schedule (if posted online, for example)
- Any other sections mandated by your department or school

Additional sections

- Writing lab location, hours, policies
- Services for students with disabilities
- Services for multilingual students
- Descriptions of major assignments
- Formatting directions for papers
- A grading rubric

When you introduce students to your syllabus, take time to point out the course objectives and how the assignments relate to those objectives. In addition, explain key terms, such as *academic writing* or *analytical essay*, that will make the formal descriptions in the syllabus more meaningful to students. Referring to the syllabus throughout the semester will help students adhere to general guidelines and the course schedule. If possible, post a copy online for easy reference.

The following sample syllabus shows one instructor's use of *The Bedford Handbook* in a twelve-week introductory composition course for traditional students. Note the course information that the instructor provides, the sequence of assignments, and the use of the handbook throughout the term.

ENG 101: College Composition 1

Meeting times:	Tu and Th, 9:00–10:30 a.m.
Instructor:	Professor Gray
Phone:	(xxx) xxx-xxxx
E-mail:	gray@yourcollege.edu
Office:	Merton Hall, Room 214
Office hours:	M, W, F, 8:00–10:00 a.m.

Course description

College Composition 1 is designed to prepare you to write essays in academic English. You will learn to plan, draft, and revise analytical and argument essays, and you will learn to write a research paper that follows MLA conventions for citations and formatting.

Course outcomes

- Students will show competence in structuring academic essays.
- Students will show competence in revising and editing their own work.
- Students will write a research paper that shows competence in using MLA conventions for in-text citations and the works cited list.
- Students will learn that writing is a collaborative effort, made stronger by peer review and feedback.

The syllabus defines course outcomes and shows students what is expected of them and what they can expect from the course.

Textbooks (available in the college bookstore)

The Bedford Reader, Tenth Edition (Kennedy, Kennedy, and Aaron)
The Bedford Handbook, Eighth Edition (Hacker/Sommers)

Assignments and grade distribution

Assignment 1 (all drafts): 10%
Assignment 2 (all drafts): 15%
Assignment 3 (all drafts): 20%
Assignment 4 (all drafts): 30%
Homework and workshop participation: 25%
A=90–100%, B=80–89%, C=70–79%, D=60–69%, F=59% or less

Attendance policy

Because this is a workshop class, your participation is important and determines your ability to succeed. You are expected to attend every class. If you must be absent, please obtain notes or missed work from a classmate. You are allowed two absences without penalty; each additional absence will reduce your final grade by one-half letter.

Grading, attendance, and makeup policies are clearly established to guide and protect students and instructors.

Late and makeup assignment policy

In general, no late assignments are accepted, and no makeup credit is granted. If you have an emergency situation, please contact me (by e-mail or phone) within twenty-four hours of the missed class session to determine whether alternative arrangements can be made. Expect to provide official documentation to prove your need to be absent.

Academic integrity

All of the work you submit in this class must be your own. When you integrate sources from other writers' work into your own papers, you must use formal citations in MLA style. Plagiarism—whether intentional or accidental—will not be tolerated and is subject to penalty. The minimum penalty is an F on the assignment; the maximum is dismissal from the college. For more information, please see the Student Guidebook, section 7.24.

The academic integrity statement makes students aware of the consequences of plagiarism, including accidental plagiarism.

Special services

The Writing Lab (Garcia Center, Room 224) offers free services to all students. I encourage you to take your drafts to the lab for additional feedback.

The syllabus points out services for students with special needs.

If you are a student with a disability, please register with the Disability Service Office (Garcia Center, Room 132) to be eligible for academic accommodations.

Important dates

Last day to add/drop this course: 9/15
Last day to withdraw with a W on your transcript: 11/4

ENG 101 Course Schedule

Week 1

Tu Introduction to the course
*   Review syllabus

Th Diagnostic essay (in class)
*   Preview the table of contents in both textbooks.

The instructor previews the handbook with the students early in the term to familiarize them with its contents.

Week 2

Tu Editing workshop: Sentence boundaries; edit diagnostic essay
*   Handbook: Fragments (19) and run-ons (20)
*   **Edited essay due at the end of class**

Th Active reading; prepare for Assignment 1
*   Reader: Chapter 1
*   Handbook: Annotating texts (4a); being an active reader (55a)

Week 3

Tu Planning and drafting; thesis statements
*   Handbook: Planning (1a-1d) and drafting (1e-1g); thesis statements (5c)

Th Revision workshop: Paragraphing; concrete details
*   Handbook: Paragraphs (3)
*   **Draft 1 due in class for the workshop**

Week 4

Tu Editing workshop: Strong verbs
*   Handbook: Active verbs (8); shifts (13); subject-verb agreement (21)
*   **Draft 2 due in class for the workshop**

Th Preview analysis assignment
*   Handbook: Writing about texts (4)
*   **Assignment 1 final draft due**

The instructor integrates the handbook at all stages of the writing process: planning, drafting, revising, and editing.

Week 5

Tu Discuss reading; prepare for assignment
*   Reader: Chapters 3 and 5
*   Handbook: Review model essay (4e and 4f)

Th Revision workshop: Integrating sources
*   Handbook: Integrating sources (52)
*   **Draft 1 due in class for the workshop**

The instructor reserves several sessions for the planning and review of each assignment.

Week 6

Tu Editing workshop: Focus on punctuation
*   Handbook: Commas (32 and 33); quotation marks (37)
*   **Draft 2 due in class for the workshop**

Th Argument and persuasion
*   Reader: Chapter 6
*   **Assignment 2 final draft due**

→

Week 7

Tu Argumentation
- Handbook: Constructing reasonable arguments (5)

Th Discuss reading; prepare for assignment
- Handbook: Review model essay (5h)

Week 8

Tu Revision workshop: Focus on argumentation
- Handbook: Supporting claims (5e); countering opposing arguments (5f)
- **Draft 1 due in class for the workshop**

Th Editing workshop: Focus on word choice
- Handbook: Wordy sentences (16); appropriate language (17); exact words (18)
- **Draft 2 due in class for the workshop**

Week 9

Tu Preview research assignment
- Reader: Chapter 11
- Handbook: Highlights of one student's research process (54b) and sample research paper (54c)
- **Assignment 3 final draft due**

Th Choosing research topics
- Handbook: Conducting research (46)

Week 10

Tu Evaluating sources
- Handbook: Evaluating sources (47)
- **Tentative thesis due**

Th Research: Visit the library to learn about databases and to find at least one source
- Bring your handbook to the library; refer to the Citation at a glance on page 552

Week 11

Tu Planning workshop: Structure
- Handbook: Review outlines (1d)
- **Outline due in class for the workshop**

Th Revision workshop: Focus on support and avoiding plagiarism
- Bring research materials to class
- Handbook: Managing information and avoiding plagiarism (48 and 51)
- **Draft 1 due in class for the workshop**

The instructor uses the handbook and model papers to introduce rhetorical strategies.

Due dates for final drafts are distributed evenly over the semester so that students have sufficient time to engage in the writing process and the instructor has sufficient time to assess papers.

Students are encouraged to use their handbooks both in and outside of class.

Week 12

Tu Editing workshop: Focus on citations
* Handbook: Review integrating sources in MLA papers (52)
* **Draft 2 due in class for the workshop**

Th Editing workshop: Focus on final edits
* Handbook: Review commas (32) and quotation marks (37)
* **Assignment 4 final draft due**

Topic 2
Designing effective assignments

The quality of student writing can sometimes reflect the quality of the assignment. Clear, meaningful assignments often lead to insightful responses and student investment. Vague or confusing assignments may frustrate students or distract them from the course's objectives, thwarting growth and achievement. The advice in this topic will help you craft assignments that provide guidance and support for your students.

Determining the objectives of an assignment

Each assignment is an opportunity for students to show what they have learned and to move toward the designated outcomes for your course. Before creating an assignment, consider your students' experience level and which of the course objectives they are prepared to fulfill. The assignment outcomes should mirror one or more of these course objectives.

Remember that students probably will not be prepared to fulfill all the objectives from the start of the term but instead will need to build skills slowly. Consider the chart on setting assignment objectives (p. 18), which shows the correlation between course objectives and two assignments in a first-year course. The first assignment, a beginning analytical essay, requires students to focus on a few basic course objectives: showing reading comprehension, writing thesis statements and topic sentences, developing paragraphs, and using the writing process. The second assignment, a final research project that is the fifth assignment in the course, shifts to more advanced course objectives. These objectives, which include evaluating sources, using citation conventions, and writing a research paper, can be accomplished only after students have developed a solid foundation in basic essay writing.

In this topic:

Determining the objectives of an assignment 17

Choosing a topic and crafting an assignment 19

Creating a sequence of steps within an assignment and integrating the handbook 20

Providing explicit instructions 21

For more information on the order of assignments, see "Determining assignment sequences" in Topic 1.

Setting assignment objectives that help students accomplish course objectives

THE COURSE **Student objectives for a first-year course**	THE ASSIGNMENTS **Student objectives for a beginning analytical essay (Assignment 1)**	
Read and show comprehension of college-level texts	Write a thesis in response to an analytical prompt	Basic skills
Formulate effective thesis statements for analytical essays	Develop the essay with paragraphs that use topic sentences to support the thesis	
Develop essays with paragraphs that support the thesis; write paragraphs that include details and concrete evidence to support generalizations (topic sentences)	Use evidence from the source text to support the thesis and topic sentences	Intermediate skills
Use the writing process to draft, revise, and edit materials	Draft, revise, and edit the paper	
	Student objectives for a research project (Assignment 5)	
Formulate an effective thesis for at least one argumentative research essay	Articulate a clear position that can be backed by research	Advanced skills
Learn to conduct research and evaluate sources	Integrate at least five credible sources in the paper	
	Draft, revise, and edit the paper	
Show skill in using MLA style for page formatting, in-text citations, and a list of works cited	Format the paper in MLA style; include in-text citations and a list of works cited	

Choosing a topic and crafting an assignment

After spending some time with your students, you will be the best judge of which topics will engage their interests and help them achieve course objectives. However, if you are just starting the semester, you may want to consult your course reader for inspiration or ask seasoned instructors in your department for sample assignments.

    Once you have determined the objectives for an assignment and chosen the topic, you will be prepared to draft the wording of the overview, the first part of the assignment. The overview typically takes the form of questions, specific prompts, or open-ended prompts.

For sample assignments, see Part III of this collection and visit hackerhandbooks.com/ teaching.

Sample assignment overviews

Questions
Write a well-focused one-to-two-page essay on the following question:
    In the article "Surfing's Up and Grades Are Down," Rene Sanchez examines the effects that computers have on college students' education and lives. **What are some of the <u>negative effects</u> that computers can have on students' academic success, according to the author? Support your answer with specific details from the text.**

Specific prompts
Develop a two-to-three-page essay on the following prompt:
    In "Weasel Words," William Lutz shows how advertisers use different types of misleading words to encourage people to buy their products. **Explain how "weasel words" used in advertising distort the truth, according to Lutz.**

Open-ended prompts
Write a six-to-eight-page research paper about a topic related to your major or intended career. The thesis of your paper should argue for a change in a specific approach or policy. Use at least five credible sources to support your thesis. Format your paper using MLA style conventions.

Novice writers working on beginning-level assignments often benefit from narrow, straightforward questions or prompts that help them focus their thoughts. Advanced writers who have had practice articulating thesis statements and developing ideas in cohesive essays can often handle more open-ended projects.

    As you draft the assignment overview, make the goals and outcomes explicit. Doing so will help you create an assignment within the students' skill range and avoid setting goals that students are not yet equipped to meet. Specifically, include key terms relevant to your course or subject, directives (such as *discuss*, *explain*, *analyze*, *argue*, *trace*, *compare*, *contrast*, and *synthesize*), and other guidelines (such as *support your response with at least three examples from the text*) that clarify the purpose of the assignment. In class, take time to explain the key terms and directives to your students, who might not fully understand what words such as *trace* or *synthesize* entail.

Creating a sequence of steps within an assignment and integrating the handbook

When you design the steps of an assignment, split the larger tasks into manageable chunks and set a due date for each step. Provide several checkpoints—especially for research projects and longer analysis papers—so that students can receive guidance from you or from their peers long before their final drafts are due. Dividing assignments into smaller steps will help students avoid both procrastination and plagiarism.

For a sample lesson, see Module 6, "Teaching citation and plagiarism."

The objectives you have already established for the project will help you determine the specific steps to assign. Depending on the assignment outcomes and your students' needs, you can set due dates for individual student tasks such as a project topic, a tentative thesis, an outline, a list of sources, and multiple drafts. The following chart provides a sample sequence of lesson steps and student tasks leading to a final research project.

Sequencing the steps of an assignment

Lesson steps	Student tasks
1. Discuss the handbook's coverage of choosing a topic and review the sample research paper.	Develop a list of three to five possible topics. Exchange feedback in a peer review session.
2. Discuss thesis statements. Practice with the handbook's print or online thesis exercises.	Settle on a topic and write a tentative thesis. Submit the thesis to the instructor for preliminary approval.
3. Discuss the handbook sections on conducting research and evaluating sources.	Find at least five sources. Bring them to class for a source-evaluation workshop.
4. Review the handbook's coverage of end citations and complete related exercises in class.	Create a list of end citations for your sources. Submit it to the instructor for feedback.
5. Review sample outlines in the handbook and discuss tips on organizing information.	Create a tentative outline. Receive feedback in a peer review session.
6. Review the handbook section on making global revisions.	Bring your first draft to class for a peer review session. Focus on global issues.

7. Discuss the handbook sections on integrating sources, avoiding plagiarism, and revising sentences.	Bring your second draft to class for a peer review session. Focus on in-text citations and sentence-level editing.
8. Ask students to share specific editing challenges. Review topics and discuss corresponding print or online handbook exercises.	Proofread your final draft and submit it for evaluation.

Providing explicit instructions

After you have drafted the assignment overview and determined the individual tasks your students will undertake, create explicit instructions for students to follow. To provide thorough support, include the following:

- An overview of the assignment (the question or prompt, including the specific objectives of the assignment)

- A brief explanation of the purpose of the assignment, showing how it relates to the outcomes of the course

- A list of the required tasks and their due dates

- Specific formatting and submission requirements, if any

- Evaluation guidelines (such as a list of the specific features of a successful paper or a copy of the rubric you will use to assess the work)

- A list of extra tips or resources, such as relevant sections of the handbook, to which students can refer during the writing process

For additional help, see the sample assignment handout at the end of this topic.

ENG 101

Assignment 2: Text Analysis Essay

Overview

In standard written English, write a two-to-three-page academic essay using MLA conventions for formatting, in-text citations, and a works cited list. Your essay should respond directly to the following prompt and **must** include properly cited **direct quotations** and **paraphrases**.

The overview clarifies the objectives of the assignment.

Prompt: In "The Roots of War," Barbara Ehrenreich compares war to "an infectious disease." How are war and disease alike, according to Ehrenreich? Is this an appropriate, reasonable metaphor?

Purpose

The purpose of this assignment is to give you practice using MLA conventions for formatting, quoting, paraphrasing, and documenting sources. This assignment builds on the basic essay-writing skills you learned in Assignment 1.

The purpose section points out the relevance of the assignment.

Due dates for assignment tasks

(Note: TBH=*The Bedford Handbook*)
9/1: Tentative thesis statement and rough outline (see 50a and 50b in TBH)
9/3: List of possible sources: must include citation information
9/5: Preliminary draft (#1): must include *at least* a thesis statement and body paragraphs
9/10: Revised draft (#2): must include the introduction, body, and conclusion
9/15: Final draft (#3)

The sequence of steps reinforces writing as a process and helps students avoid plagiarism. References to the handbook provide students with extra support.

Formatting instructions

Use MLA conventions for formatting, in-text citations, and a works cited list. Do not use a title page.

Evaluation guidelines

Excellent (A grade) papers will display the following characteristics:
- A thesis that clearly states your position on the topic
- Body paragraphs that support the thesis effectively
- Fluidly integrated in-text citations for both direct quotations and paraphrases
- An organizational pattern that advances the thesis and suits your purpose and audience
- Carefully crafted sentences in standard academic English
- An accurate works cited list and page formatting in MLA style

Evaluation guidelines set standards for achievement.

Extra help

- Review the information on integrating sources and avoiding plagiarism (see 51 and 52 in TBH).
- If you have any specific questions about your draft, stop by my office (Johnston Hall, 156-B) during my office hours or visit the Writing Center in LeCrone Hall, Room 204.

Additional tips point students to sections in the handbook and resources on campus that can help them produce successful drafts.

Topic 3
Responding to student writing

It's not *in* class but *after* class that many writing instructors begin their most demanding work—that of evaluating student papers. Your feedback is key to your students' growth as critical thinkers and effective communicators, but you have only so much time to evaluate their work. The advice in this topic can help you provide useful feedback without overextending yourself.

Understanding the purposes of responding

Many instructors, particularly those who are just starting their careers, may feel overwhelmed by the task of responding to student writing. In outcome-driven, skill-oriented programs, in particular, some instructors may feel responsible for addressing all of their students' errors with every assignment. It may be helpful to pause and reflect on the purpose of responding, which—ultimately—is to empower students to become stronger communicators. Your role as a writing instructor is not to point out every flaw in a student's paper or to edit every mistake; rather, your role is to establish (with the student's input) manageable targets for learning and growth. Keep the following points in mind as you comment on your students' drafts.

Provide students with specific tools.   Teacher responses help students build skills. Written responses on student papers and oral feedback provided during teacher-student conferences are perhaps the most beneficial when they provide specific, targeted advice that students can understand and apply immediately (in the same paper) or shortly thereafter (in a future draft or assignment). (See the sample comment on student writing on page 26.)

> Animal rights activists are often portrayed as menacing. Many times, I have noticed that their coverage of stories involving animal rights groups focuses on the activists' harsh accusations or damages to property, rather than the plight of the animals they want to protect.

Whose coverage? See 23d in the handbook. Try doing a few online exercises for pronoun reference. Also, jotting down "pronoun reference, 23d" in your editing log might prompt you to check for this error in your next draft.

Create a scaffold for future growth. It is difficult, particularly when working with novice writers, to look beyond numerous surface errors and structural flaws. Remember that writing development is slow and recursive and that you can help students learn to review their own work and introduce them to tools for revision. You can't provide your students with all the skills they will ever need as academic writers. You will best serve your students by crafting specific feedback that is sensitive to their individual abilities and needs at given stages of their development as writers.

Answer students' questions. Perhaps the most important purpose of teacher response is to provide students with answers to their own questions. Students can suggest questions about their work in cover letters or reflection journals. You also may be able to gather student questions by looking through drafts where changes are tracked electronically or editing is marked by hand. When students start the conversation and let you know when or where they would most appreciate your advice, they will be interested in and better able to apply your feedback.

Providing useful feedback

As you read over your students' drafts, keep in mind that each response is a chance for you to teach and for your students to learn. It isn't your responsibility (and some would say not your right) to copyedit a student's draft. Limit your responses to carefully chosen chunks of information that the student can digest and advice that the student will have an opportunity to follow. The following suggestions can help you focus your responses effectively.

Comment on the rhetorical situation—not just on form. To help your students become better communicators, try to vary the focus of your feedback. Resist the temptation to focus in early drafts on errors in form, such as grammatical mistakes and formatting flaws, though many students need help with these issues. First address global issues such as content, organization, and the general clarity of ideas. The following questions can help you assess global issues in your students' papers.

Addressing global issues

- Does the content meet the general requirements or scope of the assignment?

- Does the thesis or argument suit the nature of the assignment?

- Does the paper provide sufficient detail to support the thesis?

- Is the organization logical? Does the organizational pattern advance the writer's purpose and thesis?

Offer direction and praise on a few key points.   Students benefit from feedback in manageable portions that they can apply soon after they receive your comments. When providing focused direction for your students, try to praise one or two specific features of the paper and identify one or two specific areas in need of improvement. You can do this by hand or electronically with notes in the margins or at the end of the paper.

Positive comments are particularly important because they can affirm students' efforts to establish their voices as writers. Affirmation builds students' confidence and their ability to recognize strengths in their own work and that of their peers, and it guides students to use similar successful patterns in comparable writing situations. Comments that suggest revisions make students aware that they need to try different strategies in the future if they wish to communicate clearly and effectively. The following sample comments are useful models for identifying strengths as well as areas in need of improvement.

Sample comments

Sample comments on strengths

- Your introduction is strong because you present readers with a clear debate and include a thesis that anchors the rest of the essay.

- Your thesis statement works well. It responds clearly and effectively to the assignment.

- You include excellent details in your paper. Your description of the shooting accident in the third paragraph vividly supports your main idea about gun control.

Sample comments on areas in need of improvement

- Your second body paragraph would be stronger if you added a specific example of the misunderstandings between the two characters.

- Your argument begins strong but doesn't seem fully developed. To make your argument more convincing, try adding a third supporting point.

- You repeat the same information in these three sentences. Focus your reader's attention by omitting the first two.

Avoid vague language and jargon.   Comments that are either vague or too technically detailed can thwart your efforts to help your students learn and may even frustrate students because, quite simply, they will not understand what you are trying to teach them. Try to avoid using vague generalities (such as *good work*) and jargon or cryptic abbreviations (such as *awk*). If you decide to use codes or abbreviations, be sure to define them for your students. When responding to student writing, provide your students with specific praise or concrete suggestions for improvement.

See suggestions for identifying errors with handbook codes under "Managing the paper load" in this topic.

Think of yourself as part of the writer's audience, rather than the grader.   Many students enter writing classes with the preconception that they will "receive" good grades if their instructor "likes" their work. To them, instructor comments often seem to reflect arbitrary opinions instead of the observations of a trained reader. Try to build students' rhetorical awareness by writing comments from a typical reader's perspective rather than a purely personal standpoint.

Compare the two sets of comments in the box on positioning yourself as a reader. Each set attempts to provide the same advice from a different perspective. The first two comments, written in first person, may lead students to think that they are writing for one person only—you—and may dissuade them from transferring lessons to other writing situations. The second two comments, written in a more general voice, can build audience awareness because they remind students to write for a community of readers.

Positioning yourself as a reader rather than as a grader

Avoid comments that limit students' audience awareness.

- Next time, I'd like to see more specific details from the source text.
- I liked your conclusion. It left me with a sense of urgency about the problem of global climate change.

Use comments that expand students' audience awareness.

- Next time try to include more specific details from the source text so that readers will be more convinced by your argument.
- Your conclusion is strong because you leave readers with a sense of urgency about the problem of global climate change.

When correcting surface errors, begin with those that most interfere with communication.   Sometimes you may be able to comment on all of your students' errors because your students already have solid control over standard written English and make only a few mistakes. With many students, however, marking all the errors is not the best way to offer help. When you are working with less experienced students, avoid peppering their papers with your comments. Doing so leaves little time for other class preparation and often discourages students, who may feel overwhelmed by the number of comments they must address. Instead, focus on only those errors—or patterns of error—that interfere with the writer's communication. If you feel the need to let students know that their papers require significant editing, point out this fact in an end comment rather than through a legion of marks.

See "Managing the paper load" in this topic for additional ideas.

Establish goals for the next draft or assignment. In your concluding comments, present one or two realistic targets that are based on the specific feedback you've provided throughout the paper. For example, if you have suggested that the essay would have been stronger with more details, advise the student to focus on developing supporting points in the next assignment. If the sentences are missing commas after introductory elements, require the student to edit the next paper specifically for this error. Ask students to evaluate their own progress toward these goals in a cover letter accompanying future assignments.

See the sample cover letter under "Encouraging students to reflect on their own work" in this topic.

Managing the paper load

Marking papers is a time-consuming process. Even though evaluating student writing will never be as quick and easy as sending bubbled forms through a Scantron, the following strategies can help you provide thoughtful, constructive feedback in a relatively short time.

Limit the amount of marking you do. Be selective when you comment on student papers. Your role as an instructor and a coach is not to edit your students' work but to provide useful feedback that will encourage their growth. *Resist the urge to copyedit.*

- **Do an initial reading without a pen in your hand.** Before you begin marking, read through the paper once. Try to identify patterns or major features that warrant advice. Then read the paper a second time, limiting your comments to advice about those features that you identified the first time through.

- **Identify patterns of error — not all errors.** If a paper contains frequent errors of the same type, don't feel pressured to point out each occurrence. The number of marks may overwhelm both you and the student and may, in the end, thwart your effort to help the student improve sentence-level control. Instead, identify one or two examples of the most prominent errors and allow the student to find the remaining errors of the same type. Such a practice will save you time and will provide the student with a valuable skill-building exercise. If some students resist this method and look to you to correct all errors for them, explain your process and help them understand that they will learn best if they focus on a limited number of grammatical forms at one time and make their own revisions.

- **Mark errors with the symbols or rule labels used in the handbook.** The rules and patterns explained in Hacker handbooks are accompanied by letter-number codes: for example, the rule "Balance parallel ideas in a series" is S1-a in *A Writer's Reference* and 9a in *Rules for Writers*. To make error identification simple and direct, point to specific handbook rules in your comments. You can key your marks in several ways: (1) identify the error with the letter-number code of the relevant handbook section, (2) use the standard revision symbols in the chart at the end of the handbook, or (3) provide students with a key that matches sections of the handbook to your own revision symbols. (See the box "Keying editing symbols to the handbook.") Whichever method you choose, be sure to alert students to the key you are using so that they can interpret the codes. Give students some time to look over your feedback in class and to ask questions about your shorthand.

Keying editing symbols to the handbook

Using letter-number codes from the handbook

The code 32-b, written above the error, points the student to the rule "Use a comma after an introductory clause or phrase."

Even though Paulson's article provides an interesting perspective 32-b it fails

to address solutions to the problem.

Using revision symbols*

The shorthand symbol *frag* lets the student know that the sentence is a fragment in need of revision.

frag   Which the researcher should have used first.

*If you use symbols, be sure to point students to the list of revision symbols at the end of the handbook, or provide students with your own key.

Work with rubrics.   Rubrics are scoring instruments that match assignment requirements with descriptions of various levels of achievement and help establish benchmarks for your course. Holistic rubrics provide broad, general descriptions for each score or grade category. Analytical rubrics provide descriptions of particular features (such as purpose, content, organization, and sentence-level clarity) at each score or grade category, as shown in the box "Sample analytical rubric." The explanations in the rubric help clarify and create shortcuts for written feedback on student work. The best rubrics are specific to particular writing situations.

Sample analytical rubric

Feature	Excellent	Fair	Needs Improvement
Thesis/main idea	Focused, compelling, and sophisticated; provides specific direction for the reader	Focused; provides sufficient direction for the reader	Provides very little or no direction for the reader
Content and support used	Consistent use of relevant, specific examples and details from the text to create a compelling essay	Some use of relevant, specific examples and details from the text to create a compelling essay	Consistently vague or general use of examples from the text

Organization	Excellent use of paragraphs in a logical order; effective use of transitions between paragraphs and ideas	Good use of paragraphs; transitions between paragraphs and ideas may be weak; no ideas out of place	Random use of paragraphs to chunk ideas together; ideas may be out of place
Written expression	Lively, sophisticated language and sentence structures	Clear language with good control over sentence boundaries and variety	Unclear language choices; needs significant sentence-level revision

Ask students to determine areas for feedback.   In a cover letter accompanying their final drafts, students can identify one or two key features that they would like you to assess. You can provide more extensive written commentary on these features while using the rubric criteria to give students feedback on other features of the assignment.

See the sample cover letter under "Encouraging students to reflect on their own work" in this topic.

Hold student conferences.   An inexperienced writer may need more assistance than you can reasonably provide in written comments. Rather than making copious remarks on the student's paper, meet with him or her during your office hours to discuss the assignment.

Meeting with each of your students for individual conferences during regularly scheduled class time can sometimes be the best use of your time and theirs. These conference periods can serve a variety of goals: You can identify repetitive surface-level errors, check for the basic requirements of the assignment, or help the student sort out the organization of the paper. If your class is new to research writing, you can spend a few minutes with each student discussing how to integrate sources. Require students to take notes during these meetings, and briefly check their comprehension by asking them to summarize the discussion for you at the end of the session. These measures help students feel prepared to write effective essays and can shorten the time you spend commenting on final drafts.

Use a portfolio system.   Not every draft or essay students write needs to be formally graded. You can assign several essays and ask students to submit them in portfolios, collections of student-chosen writing samples. Portfolios provide students the opportunity to evaluate their own writing and to submit for assessment the pieces that they feel reflect their strongest work.

Although this system may vary depending on the course and your department's or school's requirements, most portfolio-keeping methods follow similar guidelines: The instructor asks students to collect all of their work (prewriting notes, early drafts, revisions, and final drafts) in a folder or binder. At established points during the term (at the midpoint and the end of the semester, for example), the instructor requires students to select a few of their best pieces, revise them, and turn them in for assessment. The instructor can then formally assess—with a rubric and written comments—the pieces that students have identified as their best work. The entire portfolio may receive a holistic grade based on the number and general quality of the entries, but the instructor does not need to comment on each piece of writing in the portfolio.

Encouraging students to reflect on their own work

All the time and energy you spend responding to student papers will not benefit students unless they themselves participate in the review and revision of their work. To encourage their investment in their writing and the feedback process, involve your students in activities that train them to evaluate their own work both during and after the writing process.

Provide checkpoints within the writing process.   In-class writing workshops and student self-assessments can help students learn to revise and identify errors *before* they submit their papers. These intermediate steps allow students to reflect on their writing process and submit their best work.

See the workshop ideas under "Striking a balance between global and local issues" in Topic 1.

- **In-class writing workshops.** After students have written preliminary drafts, conduct an in-class writing workshop during which students can evaluate their own work and others'. Workshops are often most productive when you structure each session with specific steps or points for review rather than merely asking students to exchange papers and comment on what they see. For instance, you might guide students through a structured self-assessment (see the next bullet point). You might also model the revision process with a sample paper while students check for the same features or flaws in their own work. (Annotated sample student papers are available on your handbook's Web site.) To maximize their opportunity for reflection and application, let students do most of the talking. Allow them to critique the sample piece, read their own work aloud, and offer advice to other students in the class.

- **Structured self-assessments.** Less experienced writers often benefit from structured self-assessments that guide them to check each key feature of their drafts. These self-assessments can be presented as checklists with simple yes/ no questions (*Does your essay introduce the source text in the first paragraph? Does your paper include a works cited page?*) or as lists of simple directives with questions (*Underline your thesis statement. Does it respond to the assignment prompt?*). You can walk students through a structured self-assessment during a workshop session, or you can require students to attach assessment forms to interim or final drafts.

Provide students with opportunities to reflect after they complete their final drafts.   Activities that encourage students to reflect on finished assignments establish a sense of continuity in the course and, more important, stress to students that each assignment is an opportunity to learn and grow. You can create activities that will focus on both sentence-level and rhetorical issues.

- **Editing journals.** To help students reflect on and learn from the surface-level errors in their papers, require them to keep editing journals throughout the semester. In these journals, students can copy flawed sentences from their writing and then correct the sentences by applying a principle from the handbook. (See the sample editing journal entry.) This activity helps students become better editors of their own work as well as learn to use the handbook on their own.

See Module 7, "Teaching grammar and punctuation," for a complete discussion of this activity and a sample handout.

Sample editing journal entry

Original sentence:

> Sedaris thinks that the things he did in his childhood was worthless compared to the things his friends was able to do.

Edited sentence:

> Sedaris thinks that the things he did in his childhood <u>were</u> worthless compared to the things his friends <u>were</u> able to do.

Rule applied:

> 21a: Make subjects and verbs agree.

- **Reflective self-assessments and cover letters.** To encourage students to think about rhetorical issues and the overall effectiveness of their work, ask them to complete open-ended, reflective self-assessments. Reflective self-assessments often work best when they are assigned at the end of the writing process (as cover letters submitted with final drafts) or after several assignments have been completed (as cover letters on portfolios of work). In these self-assessments, students can reflect on the revision process, express triumphs and frustrations, identify the specific areas with which they would like help, and establish goals for future assignments. See the sample cover letter on page 34.

Sample cover letter

Directions from the instructor: Insert a page break at the top of your final draft. On the blank page, type a brief cover letter to me that describes how you feel about this paper. Describe (1) what you think the strengths of this paper are, (2) which parts troubled you most and why, (3) why you did or did not incorporate your peer reviewers' suggestions, and (4) which parts or features of your essay you would like me to focus on in my assessment comments.

Student cover letter

Dear Professor Moore,

I think the strongest part of my paper is the introduction. I worked hard to think of a creative opening, and I like how it turned out. I also think that the thesis statement asserts my position clearly. I felt pretty confident when I was analyzing the advertisement, and I think my thesis does a good job of stating what the company's message is.

I like thinking about images and their messages, so I didn't have too much trouble with this assignment overall. I did have some trouble with the organization of my main points, though. I wasn't sure whether I should start with my analysis of the colors used in the ad or whether I should start with the paragraph about the image of the globe. My peer reviewers seemed to think that it was OK as is, so I left it in the original order.

The peer reviews were helpful. They gave me good advice about the page format and works cited list, which I have fixed for the final draft. One reviewer thought I should change the hook in my intro, but the other reviewers thought it was strong. Since these reviewers liked it and I did too, I decided to keep it. You can let me know if you disagree.

Again, I feel that I did a pretty good job on this assignment, so I don't have too many questions. I would like you to comment on the organization and let me know if you think the essay would be stronger if the points were switched around. I'd also like to know how I could improve the conclusion. I don't think the conclusion was as effective as the introduction, and I wish I could have made it better. I'd appreciate your suggestions. Thank you for taking the time to review my paper.

Sincerely,

Oscar Salamon

Topic 4
Working with multilingual writers (Teaching ESL)

Multilingual writers are enrolling in colleges across the United States in higher numbers than ever. While the increase in diversity will undoubtedly bring a welcome richness to your classroom, it may also pose instructional challenges that you may not feel prepared to handle.

As you work with multilingual writers, keep in mind that the skills they are learning take time and focus to build. Although there are few quick fixes, the advice in this topic can help you begin to address the needs of these students in your classroom.

Understanding your students' linguistic and educational backgrounds

Important to the advice in this topic is the distinction between *fluency*, or the natural use of language with appropriate levels of formality, and *accuracy*, or grammatical control over language. Some students may be highly fluent users of English with low levels of grammatical accuracy, and some students may produce technically accurate forms that sound mechanical or contextually inappropriate. Each student, depending on educational experience and linguistic exposure, will fall at a different place along the fluency and accuracy spectrums.

When you help individual students create a plan for improvement, consider these starting points and all the variables that contribute to the students' learning needs. Conduct an informal needs assessment by finding answers to questions, like the ones that follow, about your students' linguistic and educational backgrounds. You can often discover the answers by holding brief, casual conferences with your students. Asking them what they like or don't like to read in their native language can lead to important clues about their native-language literacy levels. Or you can ask them to write about their educational experiences in the diagnostic essays you assign at the beginning of the term.

What cultural and educational contexts are most familiar to my students?
Knowing your students' experiences with various educational contexts will help you predict the types of coaching they will need throughout the term. Some students have

spent many years in the US educational system. These students will probably be very familiar with the types of tasks you will assign and the classroom behaviors you will expect. They may be aware of typical expectations for collaborative activities, such as class discussions and peer reviews, and they may already be familiar with some academic genres, such as argument essays.

Students who are new to the US educational system, however, may need extra assistance in understanding expectations for classroom behavior and academic genres. The writing styles they prefer may seem ornate, illogical, or mechanical to you, and they may not be comfortable with actively engaging in discussion or group work. These students may need structured guidance for practices that other students have already internalized.

How did my students initially learn English—aurally or through formal English as a foreign language (EFL) education? Your students' original exposure to English will affect the types of rhetorical and grammatical patterns they initially produce in college writing assignments. Students who learned English primarily through conversation (whether through casual contact or secondary-level English immersion programs) often have a solid sense of style, idiom, and cadence, but they may make local errors, particularly with subtle word endings and sounds (confusing *being* and *been* or leaving off the final -*d* in a past participle or past-tense verb, for example). Typically, these students will benefit most from literacy activities that help them connect the patterns they have heard with the written forms they will be expected to produce.

Some ideas for promoting sentence-level accuracy are described in Module 7 and under "Addressing surface-level writing issues" in this topic.

Students who learned English as a foreign language in a traditional classroom setting often need fluency practice, or help learning what "sounds right" in an academic context. These students often enter college writing classes with rule-based grammatical knowledge, but they may have trouble with more contextual aspects of language: semantic boundaries (understanding the meaning of *tall* versus the meaning of *high*, for example), levels of formality, and rhetorical expectations. These writers tend to benefit less from decontextualized exercise sets and more from activities involving authentic material in context. Such activities help them learn not just how to form a particular linguistic pattern but also when and how to use it appropriately.

See "Building fluency and rhetorical awareness" and "Addressing surface-level writing issues" in this topic for activities that provide fluency practice. See also Module 7.

What are my students' native-language literacy levels? Learning about your students' native-language literacy levels can give you a sense of how quickly your students will be able to respond to writing instruction. Students who are highly literate in their native languages may enter your class with metalinguistic awareness—an understanding of how language works—and they often develop their English writing skills at a rapid pace. Students who don't have strong native-language skills may need extra time to develop as writers because they are building two skills—both English fluency and literacy in general—at once. For students in the second group, try creating activities that will build reading skills, even if your class focus is on writing. Remind these students to be patient with their own progress and to seek additional support, if possible, at your school's reading and writing labs.

How much time do my students spend speaking and hearing English every day? The answer to this question, like the answer to the previous one, lets you and your students know how quickly they might build English fluency. Some students may use English in class, at work, and at home with their siblings, spouses, or roommates. Others may listen to English only at school and may spend the rest of their time using their native languages. Naturally, the more exposure students have to comprehensible, contextualized language, the more opportunities they will have to build fluency. Remind students that their growth as writers depends on their exposure to English in all of its forms—both written and spoken—in contexts of varying levels of formality.

"Addressing surface-level issues" in this topic provides some ideas for helping students build fluency.

Promoting open classroom communication and helping students understand academic expectations

Throughout the semester, you may need to define expectations that your native English-speaking students take for granted. This is especially true if you are working with international students who have not been exposed to the academic culture of the United States or if you are working with first-generation college students. Open, friendly, and consistent communication can build the trust that is critical to the growth of these students.

Be as clear as possible with all of your students; provide models and explicit instructions. Being direct and open with students from the start can help develop appropriate classroom behaviors and can avoid miscommunication and frustration. Try not to assume that your students "should know better." Realize that some students may need instructions for classroom behaviors and procedures, such as speaking in class or working in groups, or basic formatting principles, for example where to staple a document or place their names on assignments. Provide key guidelines in writing and discuss them with the class. Be explicit when encouraging students to ask for clarification outside of class as well. For some students, contacting an instructor may seem inappropriate.

As you cover some of the model papers in your handbook or reader, be sure to point out rhetorical forms as well as formatting tips that may help your students understand your expectations. In addition, help ease the transition to the US classroom by pointing students to the ESL coverage in your handbook, which provides both linguistic and general academic help. Your handbook may include a directory of ESL boxes in the ESL menu near the end. You might also refer to section E1, "Understanding college-level expectations," in *Resources for Multilingual Writers and ESL*, a Hacker Handbooks Supplement.

See section E1, "Understanding college-level expectations," in Resources for Multilingual Writers and ESL.

Invite students to your office for conferences. If your course context and schedule allow, leave time for extra office hours to meet with those multilingual students who would benefit from one-on-one attention. Extend an invitation to stop by for individual help, which you may not have time to provide during class.

Students may assume that they are disturbing your work or that they are inconveniencing you if they contact you or visit during your office hours. International students from some cultures will not come to your office unless you take the initiative to set an appointment with them. To make students comfortable with seeking individual help, clarify your policies at the beginning of the term, and point them to the guidelines offered in section E1-e of *Resources for Multilingual Writers and ESL*.

For more advice on holding student conferences, see *"Managing the paper load"* in Topic 3.

Building fluency and rhetorical awareness

Students who write with language that seems stilted, mechanical, or illogical often just need more exposure to English. Many of these students can progress if they are given multiple models and repeated contact with standard linguistic and rhetorical patterns. To help students build fluency and rhetorical awareness, you might need to offer activities beyond the exercise sets in your handbook. The following classroom practices can help.

Engage all four linguistic modalities—even in classes designed to focus only on writing.   Create opportunities in class for your students to *listen*, *speak*, *read*, and *write* in English. Try reading aloud to your students, guiding them through a choral reading (of a poem, for instance) or assigning dictation or text-reconstruction activities in addition to the customary reading and writing tasks.

   If possible, increase your students' exposure to English by assigning tasks that will allow them to use the language outside of the classroom. For example, you might ask students to attend a talk on campus or see a play at a local theater to help them build receptive language skills.

Offer "extensive" reading and writing practice.   "Intensive" practice focuses on grammar exercises and finely edited essays. "Extensive" practice typically favors *quantity* over precision and provides multilingual students much-needed repetition with high-frequency forms. Extensive practice helps students work on general comprehension and fluency—the ability to understand and use English without translating from their native languages (the source of many transfer errors). As you design your syllabus, try to build in some extensive activities, such as keeping a journal or reading the newspaper, that allow students to strengthen their skills.

For a list of extensive language activities, see the chart in section E2 in Resources for Multilingual Writers and ESL.

Assign practice writing that will not be graded.   You might ask students to write responses to the discussion questions at the end of a textbook reading. If the reading addresses the subject of a formal essay they will write later in the term, such ungraded assignments give students the chance to grapple with the vocabulary and rhetorical patterns they will need to know when they write for a grade.

Create opportunities for self-assessment and reflection.   To lead students toward mastery of particular concepts or rhetorical patterns, build writing assignments in multiple steps that require reflection. For example, provide checklists for students to use at various stages of the writing process, assign editing logs, ask students to keep journals about their writing experiences, or ask them to submit final drafts with cover letters in which they reflect on the strengths of their papers and the challenges they faced while writing. Such reflection activities will both reinforce class topics and help students build confidence as writers.

Addressing surface-level writing issues

Assigning intensive practice—having students complete exercises and identify and correct errors in their own writing—is a good starting point for helping students address surface-level issues. But most multilingual writers will need additional practice to become effective editors. Offer print or electronic exercises that require students to fill in the blank or edit problem sentences as a first step toward mastering grammatical patterns. These exercises can help your students begin to recognize errors in other writers' work and to become comfortable with some of the grammatical terminology you use in class. Such exercises, however, should not be presented as a sole remedy or a quick fix. Once students become more comfortable with the grammatical patterns they encounter in the exercises, create opportunities for them to extend the practice to their own writing. This section presents a few strategies you can use to heighten your students' awareness of and control over English linguistic patterns.

Create awareness-raising activities.   Draw students' attention to specific language patterns with activities, such as those listed below, that focus on building linguistic awareness and receptive knowledge or on listening and reading comprehension.

- **Self-editing with attention to specific forms.** After students have completed rough drafts of an essay assignment, guide them through a self-editing exercise. With the handbook open for guidance, students can, for example, underline the subject and the verb in each sentence in their draft to check for agreement or underline every noun to determine the type of article needed.

- **Short writing assignments that require students to focus on specific linguistic forms.** You can design writing assignments that require students to practice specific grammatical patterns. For example, the prompt "Describe how you have changed since you enrolled in college" requires students to practice the use of the present perfect tense. Several similar prompts are listed in section E4-b in *Resources for Multilingual Writers and ESL*.

- **Editing logs.** For students who continue to make numerous surface-level errors, you can assign editing logs. Rather than correcting mistakes on students' essays, identify errors by highlighting or underlining them. Later, ask students to submit a log with copies of these original sentences along with corrections and explanations of the rule used to fix the sentence.

  For editing log lesson ideas and a blank log, see Module 7.

- **Dictation and text-reconstruction activities.** Another way to focus on specific forms is through traditional or modified dictation. Try replacing all the prepositions in a short passage with blank lines. Read the passage at a conversational pace, and ask students to fill in the blanks with the prepositions they hear. When the students are finished, reveal the original passage, and follow up with a discussion. Ask students to identify what was new or unexpected and to share what they learned about their own linguistic patterns. Discuss forms that were difficult to discern as well as tips for remembering specific patterns. Noticing patterns of error is the first step in self-editing.

Provide direct feedback; try not to ask what "sounds right."   When working with native English speakers, instructors often ask their students to read their own work aloud so that the students can hear their errors. This strategy typically does not work for multilingual writers. What "sounds right" to many of these students is often the source of the problem since they may not notice subtle sounds (such as *a* and *-ed*). When offering feedback to multilingual writers, provide explicit models, including sample sentence revisions, if appropriate, and encourage them to use their handbook for reference as they edit their papers. To provide focused assistance in a conference or on paper, key editing symbols to sections of the handbook.

For more on keying feedback to the handbook, see Topic 3.

Enlisting the help of other campus services

Some multilingual writers will have needs that you simply will not have time to address during class meetings and occasional office visits. If a student needs more assistance or coaching than you can reasonably offer, solicit help from the support offices on your campus.

Tutorial > Improving your academic English: A student's guide to campus ESL resources. *See your handbook's companion Web site.*

Resources for writers and tutors > Using the writing center. *See your handbook's companion Web site.*

Become familiar with the resources at your school's writing lab.   Some students will need one-on-one coaching to see a measurable improvement in their writing skills during one semester. Encourage or require these students to use the writing lab on your campus during each step of the writing process. Familiarize yourself with the lab's location, resources, and procedures so that you can provide the students with specific instructions for making the most of their visits.

Maintain an open line of communication with your school's international or multicultural student services office.   Many schools have special support offices with advising, counseling, and tutoring for international and multicultural students. Take advantage of the services at your school. With just a phone call, you might be able to arrange language tutoring or special advising for your students.

Be aware of signs of learning disabilities.   Not all linguistic concerns stem from second-language learning. Be alert for statements such as "I cannot focus," "I can't spell in my native language either," or "I have trouble organizing an essay in my native language, too." If you suspect that a student has a learning disability, seek assistance from your school's disabilities service office.

Topic 5
Addressing writing in the disciplines

by Terry Myers Zawacki

Most students in first-year composition have had little experience meeting expectations that reflect the disciplines in which their teachers have been trained. The advice in this topic, beginning with a discussion of some of the key terms associated with writing in the disciplines, is aimed at helping you prepare students for the complex writing and rhetorical tasks they will encounter in courses across the curriculum.

Understanding key terms and concepts related to writing in the disciplines

When preparing students for the writing assignments they will encounter in courses across the curriculum, it is useful to understand some of the key terms and concepts associated with writing in the disciplines, or WID, as this field of study is often abbreviated. A more nuanced understanding of WID will, in turn, help you explain to students the complexity and value of the wide range of writing and rhetorical tasks they will undertake in your course and throughout their college careers.

The term *discipline* itself is interesting to consider. While members of a discipline generally agree about core methods, genres, and preferred textual conventions, disciplines are not bound by set rules for building and writing about knowledge. Rather they can expand and change in response to new questions, methods, and social concerns.

Instructors preparing their students for assignments in various disciplines will need to address genres. Genres are much more than rigid formats into which writers pour content. Genre conventions, including rhetorical purposes, formats, and textual features such as structure and tone, differ greatly depending on the aims and motives of the discourse community—the users of particular genres of writing—and the writer's own purpose and audience. For example, a book review in an environmental science or environmental policy course might emphasize the argument the book is making related to science, whereas a book review for a literature course might focus on the author's theme, plot structure, character development, and other literary devices.

For students, learning to write in their chosen discipline occurs gradually over their undergraduate career. With practice, they learn the genres typical of the discipline and the discursive conventions—the approach, tone, structure, and style of writing appropriate for the occasion and the audience. But if students learn all of this through practice in discipline-specific courses, what can the assignments you build for one course teach them about writing in the disciplines?

Instead of teaching students rules and formats for their writing, you can help them become rhetorically aware and attentive to textual features that characterize different ways of knowing and writing in the humanities, social and natural sciences, and applied and technological disciplines such as business and engineering. These textual features include conventions for the structure of the writing (for example, organization and flow); conventions for content, such as typical thesis statements, evidence, methods, and documentation styles of the discipline; and conventions related to tone and language, including how to introduce and refer to sources, when to quote and when to paraphrase, whether to use headings and subheadings, and preferences for paragraph and sentence styles and descriptive language. (For a detailed discussion of these textual differences, see the article by Linton, Madigan, and Johnson in the list of suggested readings at the end of this topic.)

Addressing challenges related to teaching students to write in the disciplines

Because students are usually unfamiliar with the audiences and purposes assumed by their assignments in various disciplines, they may have trouble understanding the genres, conventions, and prose styles their teachers expect. Some students may lose confidence in themselves as writers. They may also become frustrated when they find that assignments of the same genre (a memo or review, for example) may be evaluated by different standards, depending on the discipline and the particular course. If students feel that the wide range of expectations they encounter when writing in various disciplines is arbitrary, they may resist your writing advice or fail to see how your assignments help prepare them for writing in other courses.

Further complicating your task are the "rules" students may have learned for generic academic writing and the attitudes of teachers who believe, sometimes along with the students, that writing should be learned "once and for all" in a composition course. Specifically, students may have trouble breaking away from some of the following:

- organizational templates, like the five-paragraph essay
- formulaic introductions, in which the thesis is only one sentence and must always appear at the end of the first paragraph
- formulaic conclusions that provide no more than a summary
- restrictions on the use of *I* in academic writing
- MLA as the preferred documentation style for the generic "research paper"

When these rules prove to be insufficient or inappropriate for the disciplinary context, students may resign themselves to the idea that teachers are all so different in their expectations that it's hard to predict what they want. (See, for example, the student attitudes reported in Thaiss and Zawacki's *Engaged Writers and Dynamic Disciplines: Reports on the Academic Writing Life*. Full publication information and a list of other readings appear on p. 48.)

One way to help students overcome these challenges is to engage them as active participants in an exploration of academic writing across the curriculum. Help them think about what teachers are expecting them to be able to do as writers and why. Provide students with opportunities to reflect on the rhetorical knowledge they already possess: What do they already know about teachers' expectations and the contexts for those expectations? How will the writing skills they've learned in one context serve them in another?

Helping students become rhetorically aware writers

Invite students to reflect on already acquired rhetorical knowledge. Active learning and reflection on learning are critical components in the transfer of knowledge from one context to another. Begin by inviting students to reflect on the rhetorical knowledge, skills, and abilities they have already acquired from previous writing experiences. Even students fresh out of high school should be able to draw on writing assignments they've completed for a variety of courses across the curriculum.

Here are some questions you might ask them to guide their self-reflection:

- What kinds of writing assignments have you been asked to do in courses across the curriculum? Which ones were most enjoyable? Why? Which were least enjoyable? Why?

- What assignments have you written with the most confidence? Why did you feel confident about them? Which ones have made you feel less than confident about your writing? Why did you feel unsure?

- How would you describe the characteristics of academic writing, as teachers have taught it or described it to you?

- What are some of the biggest differences you've noticed in the assignments teachers give and the expectations they seem to have? How would you explain these differences?

- What strategies do you use to analyze new or unfamiliar academic writing tasks and audiences?

- What writing skills do you rely on to accomplish your goals, no matter what the task?

- Have you noticed differences in the advice teachers give you regarding format, tone, and style? For example, what have various teachers told you about using *I* and contractions in your writing? Have you learned a variety of approaches toward introductions, thesis statements, and conclusions? Have teachers differed on recommended paragraph and sentence lengths?

- Do any of the differences in writing advice you've been given seem clearly related to the subject being taught? Explain.

Students will likely benefit from sharing their insights and discoveries with their peers. Explaining their experiences gives them the opportunity to analyze their own responses and expand their understanding by finding connections between their self-reflection and what they hear from their peers.

You may want to model this reflective process for your students before they begin. Think about your own academic writing experiences and how you learned to write with confidence in a variety of genres and for readers who may have had very different expectations of your writing. Students will also benefit from hearing about how you learned to become a confident writer and writing teacher.

Here are some questions to guide your own self-reflection:

- What kinds of texts do I routinely write as a scholar and a teacher? Which ones do I enjoy the most? Why?

- What writing skills do I rely on to accomplish my goals, no matter what the task?

- What strategies do I use to analyze unfamiliar writing tasks and audiences?

- How do I define academic writing based on the writing I typically do? How does my definition change when I write for different audiences and purposes?

- When it comes to stylistic conventions, is my academic writing usually formal (for example, not using *I* or contractions) or informal? How do I typically write introductions and conclusions? How do I phrase a thesis? Do my paragraphs tend to be relatively short (no more than five sentences) or longer than five sentences? Do I tend to write longer, more complex sentences, or do I prefer shorter, more concise sentences?

- To what extent and in what ways might my preferences be typical of the preferences of teachers across disciplines? How might they reflect my own disciplinary training?

Reflection helps us better understand ourselves as learners and writers: We can identify and define problems, discern patterns in learning situations and find new ways to think about them, and become agents of our own learning. Reflection is central to our ability to transfer knowledge from one context to another.

It may be helpful to create an inventory of the rhetorical knowledge, skills, and abilities your students identify in this discussion. Record their definitions of academic writing, indicating which features cut across disciplines and which ones reflect disciplinary preferences. (Be sure to acknowledge that teachers may vary, even within the same discipline, based on their own individual preferences and local contexts.) In addition, you may want to record the writing skills, abilities, and strategies your students rely on to write papers for teachers across the curriculum. To expand their rhetorical awareness, ask students to revisit the self-reflection questions and to add to these lists throughout the semester as they become more experienced writers in other disciplines.

Ask students to analyze teachers' assignments and expectations across disciplines. Early in the semester, ask students to engage in a collaborative exploration of teachers' assignments across disciplines, including yours. As with the self-reflection exercise, the goal of this exploration is to help them identify and draw on already acquired rhetorical and genre knowledge to analyze the writing task and respond appropriately. Remind them of the features that are common to academic writing across disciplines (reasoned analysis and claims supported by evidence) and those that are discipline-specific (genres, use of evidence, and textual conventions for structure and style). Here are some strategies you might consider using:

- With your students, analyze one or more of your assignments. Ask students to underline key words in the assignment that help them understand the genre (for example, literacy narrative) and the purpose of the writing, the rhetorical modes (such as narration, description), and the textual features they associate with this kind of writing. Discuss with students the contexts and mix of variables that influence your assignment and expectations, including your sense of the standards for generic academic writing, the discipline and subdiscipline in which you've been trained (for example, English and composition studies), departmental guidelines, and even personal goals you may have for them as writers. Ask them to consider how the rhetorical strategies, genre conventions, and other writing skills they are practicing in your course will transfer to the assignments they are encountering in other courses.

- Ask students to analyze the descriptions of disciplinary genres and sample student papers that appear in *Writing in the Disciplines: Advice and Models*, a Hacker Handbooks Supplement. How are the genres structured? What topics and questions do they address? Which genre features seem familiar, and which are unfamiliar? Students can work in groups assigned to different disciplines to analyze how the sample student papers reflect disciplinary genres and conventions (such as formal or informal tone; style of introduction, thesis, and conclusion; use of evidence; and documentation style).

- Ask students to perform a similar analysis on a professional piece of writing for a specific discipline. Have students describe the writer's purpose and how it relates to the rhetorical strategies the writer uses (for example, narration, comparison, or classification). Ask students if they can identify conventions for structure, content, tone, and language (see "Understanding key terms and concepts related to writing in the disciplines" on p. 41 for more on these conventions). If the writer uses the first-person point of view, have students describe the purpose and effect.

- Ask students to analyze the different expectations of teachers in courses across the curriculum by collaboratively examining assignments they have been given. This analysis should address questions such as the following:

    Why am I being given this assignment?

    What kind of writing am I being asked to do?

    What key words in the assignment help me understand what my teacher expects me to do as a writer?

    How does this writing reflect the disciplinary focus of the course and the genres typical of the discipline?

    How does this assignment fit in with other activities and writing assignments in the course?

    What do I already know how to do that will help me meet the teacher's expectations?

- Ask students to generate a list of questions they can ask teachers across disciplines about the contexts for their assignments and expectations for good writing, including those that are generic to academic writing, discipline-specific, or derived from other values and goals for writers. (For a list of questions students can ask teachers about writing in their disciplines, see "Learning from your students about writing in the disciplines" on p. 47.)

Reflecting on your own assignments and expectations

When you construct an assignment, you may have an implicit understanding of what you want students to learn, though you might not always state your learning goals and expectations explicitly. Even when you do make your learning goals explicit, you might not be fully aware of the complex mix of variables that influence your expectations, including your sense of the standards for generic academic writing, the discipline and subdiscipline in which you've been trained, departmental guidelines, and even personal preferences based on your sense of what should happen in a general composition course.

The following prompts ask you to reflect on your goals for student writers, the assumptions about academic writing that these goals represent, and the influences that shape the lessons you teach and the assignments you give. These prompts can help you identify and articulate, if you haven't already done so, how the rhetorical knowledge and writing skills students are learning in your course will transfer to the writing tasks they are given in courses across the curriculum. Finally, it's always a good practice to try out an assignment yourself before giving it to students.

Ask yourself the following questions about the assignments you give:

- What do I want students to learn by doing this assignment?
- Do my assignment goals reflect my sense of generic academic skills and rhetorical practices students must learn to be successful writers, no matter what the writing task?
- Do my assignment goals reflect learning outcomes set by the institution, the department, or the composition committee?
- Do my assignment goals reflect my sense of the different genres, formats, and documentation practices students must learn to be successful writers in courses across the curriculum?
- Do my assignment goals reflect other more personal preferences and values (for example, a sense that students need practice in writing for nonacademic audiences in nonacademic genres)?
- Will the rhetorical modes (narration, description, argument) and analytical strategies (definition, comparison and contrast, cause and effect) that I'm teaching students to write be useful to them when they write in other courses? In what way? For example, will these rhetorical modes and analytical strategies be useful when students write case studies or empirical reports based on observation and description?
- How will the genres I'm teaching students to write help them when they write in other courses? How might expectations for genres such as essays, abstracts,

annotated bibliographies, book reviews, and researched reports differ from one course to the next?

- What kinds of introductions, thesis statements, and conclusions do I want my students to write? What kind of supporting evidence do I expect my students to use? How are these expectations similar to and different from those of teachers in other disciplines?

- What tone, style, format, and other academic conventions are appropriate for this assignment and this genre of writing? To what extent are they generic to academic writing across the curriculum, and to what extent are they determined by other contexts?

- What do my students need to know about the ways in which my expectations may be similar to or different from those of teachers in other courses across the curriculum?

Learning from your students about writing in the disciplines

Addressing WID in your writing course may seem daunting. How can you begin to grasp the purposes, methods, genres, textual conventions, and other expectations for so many disciplines, courses, and teachers across your institution? It's important to remember how much your students can teach you. You can learn about the kinds of writing your students will be asked to do in their majors if you engage them as active participants in an investigation of academic writing across the curriculum. Their investigation may include interviews with professors, an analysis of their assignments, an exploration of the kinds of professional writing people do in the discipline, and the books and journals their professors write for and read. You might even want to expand this exploration to workplace documents or documents produced in social settings such as organizations and clubs.

Here are some suggestions for questions students might ask a professor in their major:

- How would you describe your discipline and your particular area of interest in the discipline?

- What kinds of questions and methods are typical of your discipline? What type of evidence is most typically used?

- How important is writing in your discipline?

- In what genres do you and your colleagues typically write and for what audiences?

- Do you or your colleagues sometimes write for audiences and in genres that are not typical of your discipline?

- Do you ever use the first-person point of view when you write? If so, when is first person acceptable?

- Does everyone in your discipline follow standard conventions and documentation styles? If so, what are they? If not, what are some of the variations?

- What do you consider to be good writing in your discipline?

For further discussion of the advice and strategies discussed in this topic, see the following readings:

Beaufort, Anne. *College Writing and Beyond: A New Framework for University Writing Instruction*. Logan: Utah State UP, 2007. Print.

Carter, Michael. "Ways of Knowing, Doing, and Writing in the Disciplines." *College Composition and Communication* 58.3 (2007): 385–418. Print.

Linton, Patricia, Robert Madigan, and Susan Johnson. "Introducing Students to Disciplinary Genres: The Role of the General Composition Course." *Language and Learning across the Disciplines* 1.2 (1994): 63–78. Print.

Russell, David. "Rethinking Genre in School and Society: An Activity Theory Analysis." *Written Communication* 14.4 (1997): 504–54. Print.

Thaiss, Chris, and Terry Myers Zawacki. *Engaged Writers and Dynamic Disciplines: Research on the Academic Writing Life*. Portsmouth: Boynton, 2006. Print.

Yancey, Kathleen Blake. *Reflection in the Writing Classroom*. Logan: Utah State UP, 1998. Print.

Modules

The modules in Part II offer strategies and lesson plans for everyday classroom use.

Notes

Module 1
Teaching thesis statements

Challenges

Unfamiliar with academic genres, novice college writers sometimes lack the rhetorical and audience awareness needed to write strong thesis statements. If they do not understand the persuasive nature of most academic works, they might write observations rather than assertions. Students who have had some high school instruction in writing thesis statements may knowingly or unknowingly resist your attempts to further develop their skills; they may assume that the instruction they received in high school is sufficient. You may see some of the following patterns emerge as students grapple with writing thesis statements:

- The thesis is too vague or broad, leading to an unwieldy paper.

- The thesis is too narrow or factual and cannot be developed into a full paper.

- Students write purpose statements (*In this paper, I will . . .*) instead of assertions.

- Students neglect to take a stance on the issue; they write observations instead of assertions.

Strategies

A clear and compelling thesis is the foundation of most college writing assignments. You can help students master thesis statements with extensive modeling and guided practice, using the following strategies:

1. Provide multiple models of thesis statements in the rhetorical style required by the assignment. When possible, present thesis statements in the context of complete texts.

2. For argument papers, use role playing so that students can practice taking a stance on an issue and arguing their points.

3. Help students frame questions that lead to an appropriate thesis statement. See the sample lesson for this strategy.

To find sample thesis statements in your handbook, see Resources at the end of this module.

Sample lesson for Strategy 3: Drafting a working thesis for an argument essay

Lesson planning:	
Sequencing:	Use this lesson near the beginning of the term, before the first essay assignment is due. You can adapt the content to fit your first essay assignment.
Student level:	This lesson targets students who are not familiar with thesis statements or who are accustomed to writing purpose statements (for example, *In this essay, I will . . .*) instead of assertions.
Learning objectives:	Students will be able to • draft a working thesis for their paper • evaluate whether sample thesis statements and other students' thesis statements contain assertions
Time required:	One session of at least fifty minutes
Materials/ resources:	Instructions for the assignment or possible topics (For this lesson, you don't need the printed instructions, but students should understand the purpose of the essay assignment before you begin.)
Lesson steps:	
	1. Begin the session by discussing the purpose of a thesis for both readers and writers. Cover the following ideas, and encourage participation as you present each point: • The thesis (made up of one or more sentences) is the most important part of the paper because it asserts the controlling idea that is proved or supported in the body of the work. The remaining ideas in the paper—especially subpoints contained in topic sentences—relate directly to this main idea. • Because it contains the controlling idea, the thesis provides necessary direction for the reader. • In the early stages of the writing process, a working thesis serves as an anchor for the writer, who can revisit the thesis throughout the drafting process to keep the content focused. 2. Emphasize the debatable nature of the thesis in most academic papers. Explain that an assertion is a stand on a particular topic, a statement that reveals a point of view that others might disagree with. It is not an observation; it is an arguable position. If some students have been exposed to purpose statements (for example, *In this paper, I will . . .*), you can also use this time to contrast such introductory sentences with assertions. For example, you can point out that others would not disagree with a statement that begins with *In this paper, I will . . .* or *This paper will show that. . . .* 3. Briefly review your assignment with students and explain that they will use this session to draft a working thesis for their paper.

→

4. Elicit subjects appropriate for your assignment, writing a few contributions on the board. Using one subject from the board as an example, ask students to suggest questions about the subject that might lead to a position. (If students have difficulty generating questions, encourage them to ask "should" questions about the subject to get started. Once they understand the objective, you can branch out into other suitable question types.) Here are a few examples:

   • Subject: global climate change

     Question: What action, if any, should the US government take to reduce global climate change?

   • Subject: childhood obesity

     Question: What should schools do to curb the childhood obesity epidemic?

5. Ask students to make an assertion by answering each question in a single complete and specific sentence. (A thesis may be longer than one sentence, of course, but this exercise is usually more successful when students focus on one sentence at this point.) Even if the students don't have strong views on the subject ask them to take a stance for the exercise. Students may need to see several models before they can write a sentence of their own. Work as a group to create one or more sample sentences, such as these, and write them on the board:

   • The US government should impose restrictions on industrial emissions to mitigate the warming effects of carbon in the atmosphere.

   • To combat the growing rate of childhood obesity, schools should organize daily physical activities, offer healthy meals in the cafeteria, and counsel parents on healthy eating habits.

6. As a class, test the sample assertions by asking if the positions can be opposed. You can ask students to offer their own opposing ideas, or you can ask them to role-play what the opposition might say. Allow students to refine the samples as necessary, making changes on the board that reflect their suggestions.

7. Give students a few minutes to write their own working thesis. After about five minutes, elicit a few examples from willing students. Again, as a class, test whether the sentences contain debatable assertions (see step 6).

8. Remind students that they can revise or change their thesis statements at any point during the writing process, especially as they find more information and further develop their own ideas.

Follow-up:	• For homework, ask students to revise their working thesis statements and submit them for preliminary approval.
	• As students develop the supporting points and body of the paper, ask them to refine their thesis by building in some direction for the major parts of the paper.
Variations:	• Once students have drafted their working thesis, conduct a peer review. Ask the peers to provide an opposing position to the thesis; if they can't, then it may need revision.
	If you are teaching online, you can create brief quizzes that ask students to test whether sample thesis statements contain debatable assertions. You can also ask students to post their tentative thesis statements on the discussion board for peer review.

Resources

Find it in your handbook	*The Bedford Handbook*, 8e	*A Writer's Reference*, 7e	*Rules for Writers*, 7e	*A Pocket Style Manual*, 6e
Planning/writing/revising a working thesis	Draft a working thesis (1c) Characteristics of an effective thesis (1e)	Drafting (C2)	Rough out an initial draft (2)	
Supporting a thesis in MLA papers	Supporting a thesis [MLA] (50)	Supporting a thesis [MLA] (MLA-1)	Supporting a thesis [MLA] (56)	Supporting a thesis [MLA] (29)
Supporting a thesis in APA papers	Supporting a thesis [APA] (56a)	Supporting a thesis [APA] (APA-1)	Supporting a thesis [APA] (61)	Supporting a thesis [APA] (35)
Supporting a thesis in *Chicago* papers	Supporting a thesis [*Chicago*] (57a)	Supporting a thesis [CMS] (CMS-1)		Supporting a thesis [*Chicago*] (40)
Writing arguments	Constructing reasonable arguments (5)	Constructing reasonable arguments (A2)	Constructing reasonable arguments (6)	
Find it on the companion Web site	**hackerhandbooks.com/bedhandbook**	**hackerhandbooks.com/writersref**	**hackerhandbooks.com/rules**	**hackerhandbooks.com/pocket**
Online exercises	Writing exercises > 1–5 and 1–6 Research exercises > MLA > 50–1 and 50–2 > APA > 56–1 and 56–2 > *Chicago* > 57–1 and 57–2	Composing and revising > C2–2 and C2–3 MLA > MLA 1–1 and MLA 1–2 APA > APA 1–1 and APA 1–2 CMS > CMS 1–1 and CMS 1–2	The Writing Process > 2–2 and 2–3 MLA > 56–1 and 56–2 APA > 61–1 and 61–2	MLA > 29–1 and 29–2 APA > 35–1 and 35–2 *Chicago* > 40–1 and 40–2

Module 2
Teaching essay structure

Challenges

Many students approach their writing assignments haphazardly, often because they don't see the value of taking the time to plan their thoughts or just don't know how. Some confess to sitting in front of their computer keyboards and rambling on with their fingers until a main idea emerges. While this brainstorming activity can help students identify and clarify their own thoughts on a topic, the resulting essay may be amorphous, with vague implications and key ideas buried within meandering examples. Students need to structure their thoughts to meet the needs of their audience.

Strategies

To help students structure their ideas effectively, plan activities such as the following that make them aware of the rhetorical features and forms their audiences will most likely expect. Use these activities early in the writing process of any project.

1. Introduce novice writers to key terms (such as *thesis*, *topic sentence*, and *paragraph*) using explicit models, such as those in your handbook.

2. Review two or more sample essays that use different organizational approaches to achieve similar goals, and discuss the features that make them effective or ineffective.

3. Assign outlines to be submitted to you or reviewed by peers before a preliminary draft is due.

4. Use graphic organizers (charts that visually represent the structure of an essay) to plan essays in class. See the sample lesson for this strategy.

To find coverage in your handbook, see Resources at the end of this module.

Sample lesson for Strategy 4: Planning an essay with a graphic organizer

Lesson planning:	
Sequencing:	Use this lesson during the planning stages of any essay assignment.
Student level:	Novice writers working on any essay or experienced writers encountering new rhetorical forms
Learning objectives:	Students will be able to • identify features of sample essays using the key terms (such as *thesis* and *topic sentence*) that have been introduced • understand the rhetorical connections between parts of an essay (such as the thesis and topic sentences) • identify the strengths and weaknesses of the organizational patterns in sample essays • plan a well-structured essay draft
Time required:	Two consecutive sessions of at least fifty minutes
Materials/ resources:	• One or more sample essays in the same rhetorical form as the assignment (Use samples from your handbook or from previous semesters.*) • A graphic organizer for each student (See Resources at the end of this module for samples.) • A slide** of the graphic organizer your students will use and a projector • Your handbook * If you have not taught the course before, you might be able to obtain samples from other instructors. ** If you don't have projection technology, you can sketch a large graphic organizer on the board.
Lesson steps:	
Session 1:	1. Introduce students to the target rhetorical form (such as a basic essay, a compare-and-contrast essay, or an argument essay) by explaining its purpose and defining key terms (such as *thesis*, *topic sentence*, *argument*, and *counterargument*) that students will need to use. Refer to the handbook for definitions and models. 2. Review one or more sample essays in the target rhetorical form, discussing the strengths of the models. Ask students to point out patterns (such as paragraph order or the order of ideas within paragraphs) and cohesive structures (such as transitional elements or strategic repetition of main ideas) that advance the purpose of the topic and help readers understand the writer's ideas.

Session 1, *continued*:	3. Using the projector (or the board), introduce the graphic organizer that your class will use. Ask students to suggest ways to fill in the graphic organizer with information from the sample essay. Point out the consistency between the thesis and the topic sentences, for example, so that students can visualize the rhetorical connections. 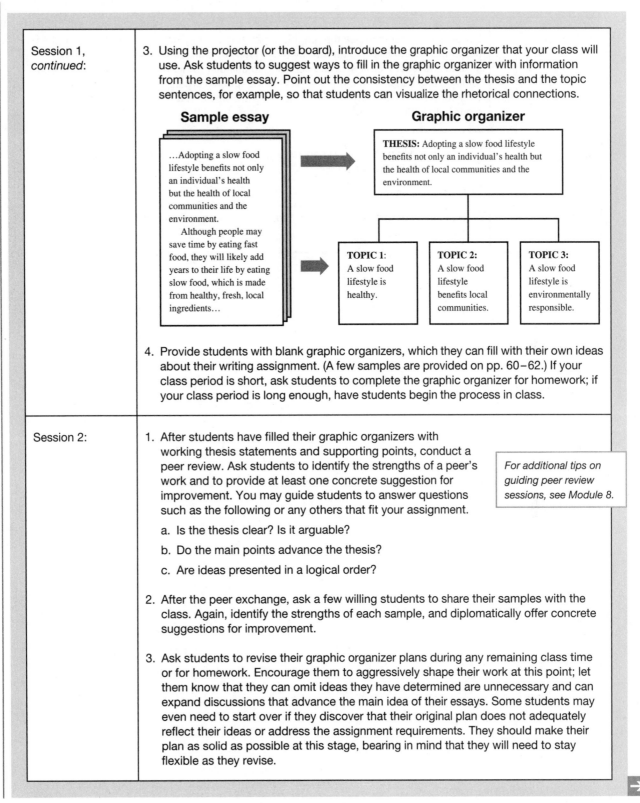 4. Provide students with blank graphic organizers, which they can fill with their own ideas about their writing assignment. (A few samples are provided on pp. 60–62.) If your class period is short, ask students to complete the graphic organizer for homework; if your class period is long enough, have students begin the process in class.
Session 2:	1. After students have filled their graphic organizers with working thesis statements and supporting points, conduct a peer review. Ask students to identify the strengths of a peer's work and to provide at least one concrete suggestion for improvement. You may guide students to answer questions such as the following or any others that fit your assignment. *For additional tips on guiding peer review sessions, see Module 8.* a. Is the thesis clear? Is it arguable? b. Do the main points advance the thesis? c. Are ideas presented in a logical order? 2. After the peer exchange, ask a few willing students to share their samples with the class. Again, identify the strengths of each sample, and diplomatically offer concrete suggestions for improvement. 3. Ask students to revise their graphic organizer plans during any remaining class time or for homework. Encourage them to aggressively shape their work at this point; let them know that they can omit ideas they have determined are unnecessary and can expand discussions that advance the main idea of their essays. Some students may even need to start over if they discover that their original plan does not adequately reflect their ideas or address the assignment requirements. They should make their plan as solid as possible at this stage, bearing in mind that they will need to stay flexible as they revise.

Follow-up:	Encourage students to use the graphic organizers as they begin drafting. Remind them not to feel bound to this plan as they make later revisions, but encourage them to structure at least their first draft according to this plan, which has been peer-reviewed for logic and sense. Ask students to bring the graphic organizers to future revision workshops to refer to if necessary. Students should submit their graphic organizers along with their final drafts.
Variations:	• After introducing graphic organizers, ask students to create their own for each assignment instead of an outline. ⬛ If you are teaching online and your students use compatible word processing programs, you can provide sample essays and corresponding graphic organizers with tables or text boxes to fill in. Students can peer-review each other's work using comment fields.

Resources

Find it in your handbook	*The Bedford Handbook,* 8e	*A Writer's Reference,* 7e	*Rules for Writers,* 7e	*A Pocket Style Manual,* 6e
Planning and outlining	Rough out a first draft (1c, 1e to 1g)	Drafting (C2)	Rough out an initial draft (2)	
Thesis statements in MLA papers	Supporting a thesis (50)	Supporting a thesis (MLA-1)	Supporting a thesis (56)	Supporting a thesis (29)
Thesis statements in APA papers	Supporting a thesis (56a)	Supporting a thesis (APA-1)	Supporting a thesis (61)	Supporting a thesis (35)
Thesis statements in *Chicago* papers	Supporting a thesis (57a)	Supporting a thesis (CMS-1)		Supporting a thesis (40)
Paragraphing and writing topic sentences	Build effective paragraphs (3)	Writing paragraphs (C4)	Build effective paragraphs (4)	
Constructing arguments	Constructing reasonable arguments (5)	Constructing reasonable arguments (A2)	Constructing reasonable arguments (6)	
Find it on the companion Web site	**hackerhandbooks.com/ bedhandbook**	**hackerhandbooks.com/writersref**	**hackerhandbooks.com/rules**	**hackerhandbooks.com/pocket**
Online exercises	Writing exercises > 1–3 Research exercises > MLA > 50–1 and 50–2 > APA > 56–1 and 56–2 > *Chicago* > 57–1 and 57–2	Composing and revising > C2–2 and C2–3 MLA > MLA 1–1 and MLA 1–2 APA > APA 1–1 and APA 1–2 CMS > CMS 1–1 and CMS 1–2	The Writing Process > 2–2 and 2–3 MLA > 56–1 and 56–2 APA > 61–1 and 61–2	MLA > 29–1 and 29–2 APA > 35–1 and 35–2 *Chicago* > 40–1 and 40–2

Sample graphic organizer for a basic essay

These boxes are meant to help you organize your thoughts. They do not necessarily represent individual paragraphs.

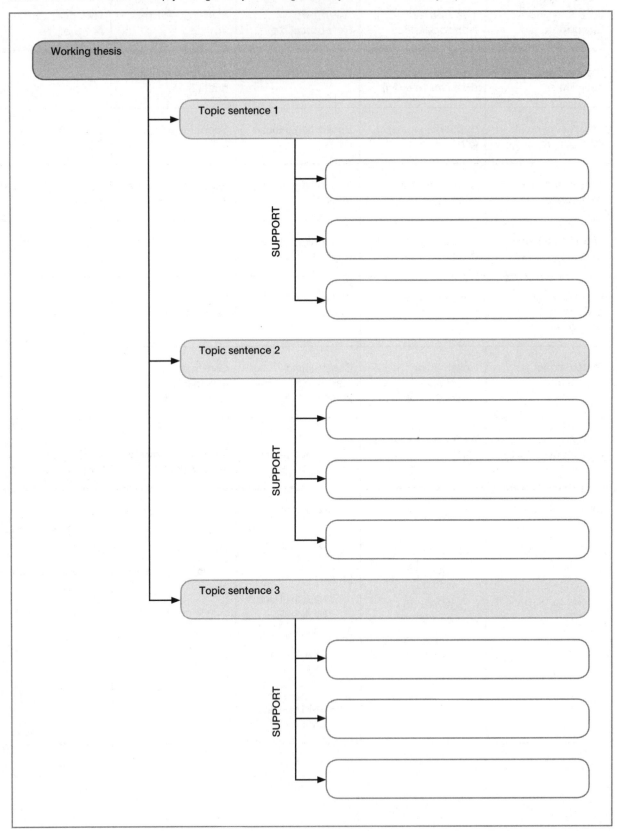

Sample graphic organizer for a compare-and-contrast essay

These boxes are meant to help you organize your thoughts. They do not necessarily represent individual paragraphs.

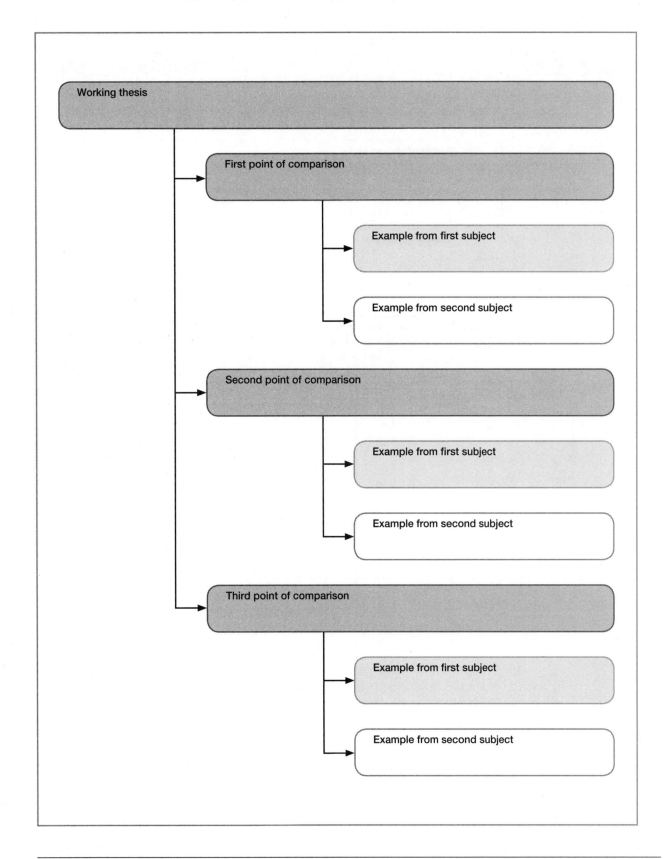

Sample graphic organizer for an argument essay

These boxes are meant to help you organize your thoughts. They do not necessarily represent individual paragraphs.

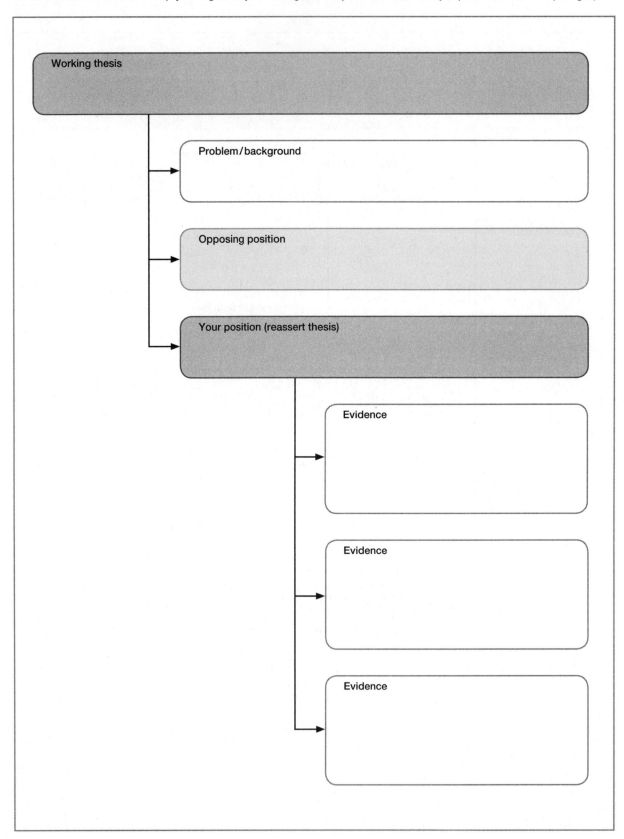

Working thesis

Problem/background

Opposing position

Your position (reassert thesis)

Evidence

Evidence

Evidence

Module 3
Teaching paragraphs

by Elizabeth Canfield

Challenges

Teaching paragraphs can be challenging for us; as experienced writers, we may have internalized essay and paragraph structure. Because we understand the relationship between organization and meaning and can anticipate readers' needs, we may struggle to explain effective paragraphing techniques to students who are not as aware of their audience and how to reach them. Especially in a freshman writing class, students will have varying levels of experience with thinking about or writing cohesive and organized paragraphs.

When paragraphing, students might face some of the following challenges:

- Readers expect paragraphs to guide them from one clearly stated and defended idea to the next. If students write without a sense of organization and lump their prose into paragraphs intuitively, readers will find those paragraphs disorganized and confusing. What seems natural to the writer may not be logical for the reader.

- Many students have internalized a five-paragraph essay form that inhibits their ability to write expansive or detailed pieces; they may not understand how to break long discussions into more than three body paragraphs.

- Some students will produce pieces of writing with no paragraphs at all.

Strategies

Although at first it might seem desirable to teach students what paragraphs are (by showing them models of paragraphs with topic sentences and supporting sentences), it might not be as beneficial as helping students see the relationships between ideas and how ideas can be grouped together. The following strategies can help students grasp how paragraphs work:

1. Help students understand that they should not think of paragraphs as a template into which they must force their ideas.

2. Discuss paragraphing in the context of a larger conversation about how structure reveals and reinforces relationships between ideas (from the sentence level to the essay level).

3. Take a student draft and remove the paragraph structure. Ask students to read through the draft without paragraphs and think about where breaks and transitions would help readers and the writer. See the sample lesson for this strategy.

Sample lesson for Strategy 3: Paragraphing workshop

Lesson planning:	
Sequencing:	Students should have already completed at least one draft of their first writing assignment.
Student level:	Novice writers, though more experienced writers could also benefit from this lesson
Learning objectives:	Students will be able to • discuss the purposes of paragraphs in writing • practice writing topic sentences and subordinate and coordinate ideas in the context of a draft-in-progress
Time required:	Two sessions of at least fifty minutes
Materials/ resources:	• Overhead projector (and transparency) or laptop projector • Bring a sample student essay or reader selection to Session 1 (see Session 1, step 1). If possible, have an electronic file or transparency available for projection. Students should come to Session 2 with an essay draft. The suggested activity for Session 2 will work best if students write on similar topics or in response to the same readings.

→

Lesson steps:	
Session 1:	1. Provide students with a sample paper or a reader selection. Ask them to identify a paragraph they find effective. Give them time to write a short response explaining their choice. (If time is short, this step can be completed as homework for Session 1.) 2. In small groups, have the students read their favorite paragraphs aloud to their peers and briefly explain their choice. Each group should then choose one paragraph to focus on. Each group should discuss the following questions about the paragraph they've chosen: • Why did you choose this paragraph? • How does the writer group ideas together? Describe the order of the sentences within the paragraph. How does the paragraph begin? How does it end? • How do the sentences work together within the paragraph? What is each sentence's "job" for creating meaning? 3. Ask groups to share their responses with the class. (If projecting the paragraph is not an option, make sure every student has a copy of the essay.) 4. To prepare for Session 2, provide students with a handout that lists some characteristics of topic sentences. Students should add to the list and match up each characteristic with an appropriate topic sentence from the paragraphs discussed in Session 1. To get your students started, you can list a few of the following characteristics: (a) topic sentences don't have to be the first sentence of a paragraph; (b) topic sentences can express a question, which the rest of the paragraph answers; (c) topic sentences can express an opinion, a fact, or an attitude, which other sentences support or discuss; (d) topic sentences can present a problem, which the paragraph addresses; and (e) topic sentences can summarize what other sentences explore in detail.
Session 2:	1. Take a few minutes to discuss the characteristics and examples students gathered in preparation for this session. Record some characteristics on the board. 2. To begin the topic sentence workshop, ask students to take out their drafts. (The following suggested steps work best if students have written on the same topic or in response to the same readings.) • Ask students to write a possible topic sentence for a paragraph for their essay-in-progress on a separate sheet of paper, using their topic sentence handout and the examples on the board to guide them in creating their topic sentence. • Collect the sheets of paper, and using either the board or a projected laptop, display one student-generated sample topic sentence. (The selected topic sentence should be strong enough to provide clues about the purpose and direction of the paragraph. If the class is writing on a variety of topics, however, the writer of the sample topic sentence may want to provide some additional context about the essay.) • Ask the class to brainstorm sentences that would surround or follow the sample topic sentence, and write them on the board. • Once the paragraph is drafted, ask the class if any of the sentences can be moved around to convey meaning more clearly and effectively.

Session 2, *continued*:	• Process questions: Ask students why they made the choices that they did with *what* they said and *how* they said it.
	• Repeat the steps in this list at least one more time.
	3. Once students have had some practice with the previous exercise, ask them to do one of the following:
	• Repeat the previous exercise on their own with one of the sentences that they generated earlier in the session.
	• Revise an existing paragraph in their essay draft to reflect a strong topic sentence and well-arranged and well-crafted subordinate/coordinate sentences.
Follow-up:	It is helpful to repeat this lesson more than once and to explain the relationship of this exercise to other exercises focused on structuring the essay as a whole.
Variations:	• Session 2 can focus on a later draft. Turn the topic sentence workshop into a revision workshop using paragraphs that students have already generated for their essay. Have them consider the following questions: (1) Look at key words in the topic sentence. What does the topic sentence promise readers that the paragraph will be about? (2) Does the paragraph fulfill that promise? If so, how? If not, where does it fall short? (3) How might the paragraph be revised? (4) What are the strengths and limitations of the draft topic sentence, from a writer's and a reader's point of view?
	🖥 If your course is conducted online, discussion boards or blogs can be a good setting for Session 1. Session 2 requires a collaborative writing space (such as *Google Docs*).

Resources

Finding it in your handbook	*The Bedford Handbook,* 8e	*A Writer's Reference,* 7e	*Rules for Writers,* 7e	*A Pocket Style Manual,* 6e
Planning and drafting	Exploring, planning, and drafting (1) Rough out a first draft (1e to 1g)	Planning (C1) Drafting (C2)	Generate ideas and sketch a plan (1) Rough out an initial draft (2)	
Making global revisions	Make global revisions (2)	Revising (C3)	Make global revisions (3)	Checklist for global revision
Paragraphing: focus	Focus on a main point (3a)	Focus on a main point (C4-a)	Focus on a main point (4a)	
Paragraphing: development	Develop the main point (3b)	Develop the main point (C4-b)	Develop the main point (4b)	
Paragraphing: patterns of organization	Choose a suitable pattern of organization (3c)	Choose a suitable pattern of organization (C4-c)	Choose a suitable pattern of organization (4c)	
Paragraphing: coherence	Make paragraphs coherent (3d)	Make paragraphs coherent (C4-d)	Make paragraphs coherent (4d)	
Paragraphing: length	If necessary, adjust paragraph length (3e)	If necessary, adjust paragraph length (C4-e)	If necessary, adjust paragraph length (4e)	

Module 4
Teaching argument and counterargument

by Nancy Sommers

Challenges

Learning to argue a thesis and support it with appropriate evidence requires students to establish a position, anticipate counterpositions, and persuade readers. If students don't understand the persuasive nature of academic writing, or if they think of argument as a debate with winners or losers, they may have difficulty grasping the conventions and expectations of academic argument. Some specific challenges you might encounter include the following:

- Students are reluctant to take a stance on an issue.
- Students confuse opinions with positions.
- Students are unfamiliar with the language of argument: thesis, claim, evidence, counterargument.
- Students are unfamiliar with strategies for developing an argumentative thesis.
- Students believe that one piece of evidence "proves" a writer's point of view.
- Students are inexperienced with summarizing, paraphrasing, quoting, and interpreting evidence.
- Students believe that introducing counterarguments will weaken their positions.
- Students come from cultures that value different modes of argumentation.

For further discussion of working with multilingual writers, see Topic 4.

Strategies

Help students become comfortable with academic arguments by providing authentic models of student and professional arguments. Give them plenty of practice in recognizing the elements of argument—thesis, claim, evidence, and counterargument—and clear guidelines for reading and interpreting the structure of arguments. Introduce students to the idea of constructing and evaluating their own arguments with the following strategies:

1. Conduct thesis workshops. Ask students to draft a thesis. Then have them brainstorm counter thesis statements to illustrate that effective argumentative thesis statements can be opposed.

2. Have students give two-minute oral arguments to support a stance they've taken. Ask peers to propose counterarguments. Help students understand that readers will make up their minds after listening to all sides of an argument.

3. Provide models of student and professional arguments to illustrate the elements of argumentation. Focus discussion on the questions each writer asks; the thesis being argued; the evidence each writer analyzes; and the counterarguments that are presented. See the sample lesson for this strategy.

Sample lesson for Strategy 3: Learning to analyze academic arguments

Lesson planning:	
Sequencing:	Use this lesson to introduce academic argument.
Student level:	This lesson targets students who are unfamiliar with the elements of academic argument. Students will need some prior experience identifying thesis statements, topic sentences, and evidence in written texts. They should also have had experience summarizing texts.
Learning objectives:	Students will be able to • read and evaluate an argument • identify the elements of an argument • question the assumptions of an argument • engage with the evidence of an argument • anticipate and address counterarguments
Time required:	Two sessions of at least fifty minutes
Materials/ resources:	The handbook

Lesson steps:	
Preparation for Session 1:	1. Ask students to read Jamal Hammond's argument, "Performance Enhancement through Biotechnology Has No Place in Sports," a student essay on their Hacker handbook's companion Web site. (See Resources on p. 74 for the URL. Some Hacker handbooks also include this essay in the text.) 2. Ask students to write a one-paragraph summary of Hammond's argument. Explain that summarizing an argument helps the reader articulate an author's key points. 3. Ask students to e-mail their summaries to you before class and to bring a copy of their summaries to Session 1.
Session 1:	1. Point out that the class will be learning about argument by taking a close look at Hammond's thesis, assumptions, and use of evidence and counterargument. With their summaries in hand, ask students to respond generally to the following questions: <ul><li>What debate has Hammond entered?</li><li>What is Hammond's position in this debate?</li><li>What key claims does he make to support his position?</li></ul> 2. Have students turn to Hammond's essay. Briefly review the purpose of thesis statements with students. Remind them that a thesis can be an answer to a question posed, the resolution of a problem identified, or a position taken in a debate. Point out how each sentence in Hammond's introduction leads readers to his thesis. Focus students' attention on Hammond's thesis by asking the following questions: <ul><li>How does Hammond's introduction identify a problem?</li><li>According to Hammond, why should readers care about this problem?</li><li>What question is Hammond asking about performance-enhancing substances?</li><li>What are Hammond's assumptions about the role of "fair play" and "hard work" in sports? How do these assumptions shape his argument?</li><li>How does his thesis show that he is taking a position in a debate?</li></ul> 3. Focus students' attention on Hammond's use of counterargument. For a quick review, ask students to define *counterargument*. Point out to students that writers show themselves as more reasonable and credible thinkers if they acknowledge counterpositions. Then, ask students to evaluate Hammond's counterargument. They should support their answers with specifics from Hammond's essay. To aid them in their evaluation, have them address the following questions: <ul><li>What language does Hammond use to introduce a counterposition?</li><li>How does the inclusion of a counterargument strengthen his position?</li><li>How does mentioning the counterargument make him seem more reasonable and knowledgeable?</li><li>How does he respond to the counterposition?</li><li>How would Hammond's argument have been weakened if he hadn't included a counterposition?</li></ul>

Session 1, *continued*:	4. Focus students' attention on Hammond's evidence. First, ask students to name the types of evidence writers often use to support their arguments: facts, statistics, examples and illustrations, and expert opinions. Remind students of the importance of documenting sources to give credit to authors. Then, ask students to evaluate the persuasiveness of Hammond's support by answering the following questions about his use of evidence: • How does Hammond use evidence to support his claims? • How does Hammond interpret his evidence? Since evidence doesn't speak for itself, what would be missing if Hammond presented evidence without interpretation? • Imagine removing one piece of evidence from Hammond's essay. How would that absence weaken the essay? • Does Hammond provide sufficient evidence? If not, what kind of evidence is missing?
Preparation for Session 2:	1. Ask students to enter the debate with Hammond's argument by annotating his essay. 2. Have students propose counterarguments by questioning Hammond's thesis, assumptions, evidence, or reasoning. 3. Ask students to develop their counterpositions with these templates: "Some readers might point out . . ." "Critics of this view argue . . ." "Hammond's argument fails to recognize . . ."
Session 2:	The goal of this exercise is to model for students how arguments grow out of lively conversations between writers and readers. 1. Begin the session by asking three or four students to write their counterarguments on the board. Remind students of the important role that counterargument plays in building strong argument essays. Some students will question Hammond's assumptions about sports. Other students will object to his "either/or" reasoning and propose ways to modify his position. 2. Put students into peer groups and assign some groups to support Hammond's thesis (that any form of biotechnology should be banned from competitive sports) and some to challenge it. With the group's assignment in mind, each student should first work alone to pose a question and write an argumentative thesis in response to that question. The group should then discuss these thesis statements and test them by thinking about objections readers might raise. Ask each group to appoint a spokesperson to record the group's thesis statements and possible challenges to those statements. The purpose of the peer group discussion is to help students learn to (a) develop a thesis in response to a question; (b) listen emphatically; (c) summarize, fairly and credibly, the views of others; (d) raise and respond to different sides of an argument. The peer discussion will also allow students to practice taking a stance, moving beyond opinion to argument, and learning how arguments evolve from lively conversations. Bring the class back together by asking each spokesperson to present the group's thesis statements and challenges to those statements. 3. Pull together the lessons of the two sessions by giving students five or ten minutes to write in response to this prompt: *What have you learned about argument and counterargument?* Collect the students' reflections and review them to see whether students have grasped the major concepts.

Follow-up:	1. Provide students with the following guidelines for constructing and strengthening their own arguments:
	• Identify a debatable issue.
	• Examine the issue's social and intellectual contexts.
	• Develop a thesis that clearly states your position on the issue.
	• Support your thesis with evidence and persuasive lines of reasoning.
	• View your audience as a panel of jurors.
	• Anticipate objections; counter opposing arguments.
	• Quote opposing views with fairness and accuracy.
	• Cite and document sources.
	2. Use this lesson as groundwork for peer review of argument essays. Have students apply questions along these lines to each other's drafts:
	• What debate has the writer joined in this draft? What are the various positions in this debate?
	• How does the writer's thesis answer a question posed, resolve a problem, or take a position?
	• What assumptions is the writer making?
	• How has the writer anticipated and countered opposing arguments?

Resources

Find it in your handbook	*The Bedford Handbook,* 8e	*A Writer's Reference,* 7e	*Rules for Writers,* 7e	*A Pocket Style Manual,* 6e
Active reading	Read actively: Annotate the text (4a)	Read actively: Annotate the text (A1-a)	Read actively: Annotate the text (5a)	
Analysis and critical thinking	Analyze to demonstrate your critical thinking (4d)	Analyze to demonstrate your critical thinking (A1-d)	Analyze to demonstrate your critical thinking (5d)	
Constructing arguments	Constructing reasonable arguments (5)	Constructing reasonable arguments (A2)	Constructing reasonable arguments (6)	
Evaluating arguments	Evaluating arguments (6)	Evaluating arguments (A3)	Evaluating arguments (7)	
Sample argument paper	Hammond, "Performance Enhancement through Biotechnology Has No Place in Sports" (5h)	Jacobs, "From Lecture to Conversation: Redefining What's 'Fit to Print'" (A2-h) [Sixth Edition: Hammond, "Performance Enhancement through Biotechnology Has No Place in Sports" (A2-h)]	Jacobs, "From Lecture to Conversation: Redefining What's 'Fit to Print'" (6h) [Sixth Edition: Hammond, "Performance Enhancement through Biotechnology Has No Place in Sports" (47h)]	
Find it on the companion Web site	**hackerhandbooks .com/ bedhandbook**	**hackerhandbooks .com/writersref**	**hackerhandbooks .com/rules**	**hackerhandbooks .com/pocket**
Sample argument paper	Model papers > MLA Argument Papers > Hammond, "Performance Enhancement through Biotechnology Has No Place in Sports"	Model papers > MLA Argument Papers > Hammond, "Performance Enhancement through Biotechnology Has No Place in Sports" Jacobs, "From Lecture to Conversation: Redefining What's 'Fit to Print'"	Model papers > MLA Argument Papers > Hammond, "Performance Enhancement through Biotechnology Has No Place in Sports" Jacobs, "From Lecture to Conversation: Redefining What's 'Fit to Print'"	Model papers > MLA Argument Papers > Hammond, "Performance Enhancement through Biotechnology Has No Place in Sports" Jacobs, "From Lecture to Conversation: Redefining What's 'Fit to Print'"

Module 5
Teaching students to conduct research and evaluate sources

Challenges

Many students enter college without experience in conducting research and working with sources at the college level. If they have written research papers in the past, the guidelines for these assignments were probably less rigorous than the demands of college research assignments, and students may not have ventured beyond a quick search on the Web. You will likely encounter the following challenges when you give research assignments:

- Students don't know how to pose a research question; research to them is an accumulation of information rather than evidence to support their own arguments.

- Students use only Internet search engines like *Google* to find sources for their projects.

- Students are unfamiliar with or even intimidated by the search tools and resources at the library, including online databases.

- Students don't have practice evaluating sources and thus are not able to distinguish between credible and unreliable sources.

- Students do not recognize bias in the sources they find.

Strategies

Students can benefit from guided exercises and tutorials that provide them with authentic, hands-on research experience. The following strategies can help you guide students through the process of finding, evaluating, and documenting sources:

1. Introduce students to the resources available at your school and show them how to search online databases. If possible, enlist the help of a reference librarian. Be willing to spend an entire class period to orient students.

2. Review the handbook's discussion of evaluating sources, including checklists on "Evaluating all sources" and "Evaluating Web sources." Using a common source, go through the appropriate checklist as a class.

3. Practice information gathering in a real-life scenario. For example, provide a sample thesis and ask students to locate a reliable electronic source. Have students explain how the source might support the sample thesis.

4. Practice creating sample works cited entries (or end citations) together. Help students navigate the handbook's citation directories and models.

5. Assign annotated bibliographies, which require students to find sources to support their argument, evaluate the sources in writing, and create an appropriate works cited list, references list, or bibliography. The sample lesson provides specific guidelines for applying this strategy.

Sample lesson for Strategy 5: Annotated bibliography

Lesson planning:	
Sequencing:	Use this lesson after students have learned about basic research strategies and have settled on a research question but before they complete any drafts.
Student level:	Students should have already had experience with writing thesis statements and paragraphs, writing about texts, and constructing arguments.
Learning objectives:	Students will be able to • evaluate sources using the guidelines in the handbook • navigate the appropriate documentation style section in the handbook to create end citations • begin an annotated bibliography
Time required:	Two sessions of at least fifty minutes

Materials/ resources:	Session 1 • The handbook • Source texts (Each student should bring three to five scholarly sources that fit his or her research project.) Session 2 • The handbook • At least one sample annotated bibliography entry. Provide copies for each student, or create a transparency or an electronic copy to project on the board. • Ask students to bring bibliographic information for source texts.

Lesson steps:

Preparation:	1. Guide students through the process of choosing a topic and research question for your assignment. Assignments will vary depending on the goals of your course and department. The annotated bibliography can be used as a preliminary step toward a more extensive research paper, or it can serve as the final product of each student's research. 2. If possible, take a tour of your school's library or ask a librarian to introduce the search tools available on your campus. Many first-year and even second-year students will need help accessing academic articles through online databases. For background reading, assign your handbook's coverage of finding and evaluating sources. Let students know that they can turn to you, the librarian, and their handbook for help with understanding what constitutes a scholarly or academic source. 3. After students have learned about your library system's search tools, ask them to bring three to five scholarly sources on their research topic to Session 1. In preparation, have them review your handbook's coverage of evaluating sources.
Session 1:	1. Discuss the handbook's coverage of evaluating sources, pointing out questions that students can ask to determine whether their sources are scholarly and credible. Focus on questions that can help students evaluate any source. Assessing an argument • What is the author's central claim or thesis? • How does the author support this claim—with relevant and sufficient evidence or only with anecdotes or emotional examples? • Are statistics consistent with those you encounter in other sources? Have they been used fairly? Does the author explain where the statistics come from? • Are any of the author's assumptions questionable? • Does the author consider opposing arguments and refute them persuasively? • Does the author fall prey to any logical fallacies?

Session 1, *continued*:	Checking for signs of bias • Does the author or publisher endorse political or religious views that could influence the argument? • Is the author or publisher associated with a special-interest group, such as Greenpeace or the National Rifle Association, that might present only one side of an issue? • Are alternative views presented and addressed? How fairly does the author treat opposing views? • Does the author's language show signs of bias? 2. If your students will be conducting research on the Web, guide them to specific questions they should ask to evaluate Web sources, including those about *authorship*, *sponsorship*, *purpose* and *audience*, and *currency* discussed in your handbook. Remind students that if an article's authorship and sponsorship are unknown, the source might not be credible or scholarly. 3. Have a willing student share his or her research question and purpose and describe a sample source. Ask the student to provide basic information about the search process and source text: • How was the search performed (for example, with a *Google* search, with the library's online databases)? • What is the title of the text? • Who is the author? Does the author have any credentials? 4. With the help of the class, discuss the credibility of the source. Even though students will not have read the source, they should still be able to determine whether the source warrants further reading or is unsuitable for inclusion in the research project. Consider discussing answers to the following questions: • Was the student's search process likely to turn up scholarly sources? • Does the title seem to be scholarly? • Do the author's credentials qualify him or her to write on the topic? 5. Divide students into small groups (three or four students each) to evaluate the sources they have brought to class. Encourage them to follow the same process you used in evaluating the sample document and to use the handbook's guidelines for evaluating sources. Offer guidance to students who disagree about the credibility of a source or who have additional questions. If students discover that some of their sources are not credible or appropriate, let them know that they still have time to find other sources to include in their projects. 6. For homework, ask students to replace any sources their group rejected as not credible or not scholarly. To begin working on their annotated bibliographies, students should bring to Session 2 the bibliographic information for all sources they are considering.

| Session 2: | 1. Begin this session by explaining the purpose of the annotated bibliography assignment: to provide students with authentic practice conducting college-level research, to help them learn about a topic of their choice, to give them practice summarizing sources, to help them figure out how sources relate to their topic and their own position, and to give them experience with evaluating and documenting the sources they find. If you plan to use the annotated bibliography as a preliminary step in a larger research project, you can also explain that this assignment will help them manage both their time and their information as they begin their research. |

2. Distribute or project a sample entry from an annotated bibliography and introduce its parts: the citation and the annotation. The annotation may take many forms, so you will need to specify what each entry should include. Usually three to seven sentences long, annotations often include one or more of the following points, depending on your course context and assignment goals:

> *For a list of sample annotated bibliographies on your handbook's companion Web site, see Resources at the end of this module.*

- A brief summary of the source

- An analysis or evaluation that identifies biases, explains how the source fits within the field, or compares the source to the others in the bibliography

- An explanation of the source's function in the research project

3. Ask a willing student to share a sample source. Using the handbook as a guide, work with the class to create an end citation for the source. Students may need help navigating the MLA, APA, or *Chicago* style section of the handbook and identifying the source type and corresponding citation model. Many students won't recognize the difference between a Web site and an article posted on a Web site, for example, and will need specific guidance.

4. Work with students to write a sample annotation. Ask the student who contributed the source to provide general information about the text for the class to work from.

5. After the students have constructed a model citation and annotation, give them time to draft an annotated citation for one of their own sources. (Some students will finish more quickly than others; ask these students to continue drafting citations and annotations for their other sources.)

6. After about ten minutes, ask students to share one of their annotations with one or more peers and to note strengths in the samples of their peers.

7. Before the class period ends, ask a few students to comment on the strengths they noticed in their peers' work. With the writers' permission, share a few particularly strong annotations with the class. (Some writers may be shy about reading their own work. You can ask another student to read the entry aloud, or you can offer to read it to the class.)

8. Wrap up by summarizing the features of an annotated bibliography and the strengths of the samples noted in class. Assign a draft of the annotated bibliography for homework.

Follow-up:	Conduct peer reviews of full annotated bibliographies. You can devote an entire class period to the peer review, or you can ask students to share a few entries during one segment of the class period.
Variations:	If your school has such resources, consider reserving a computer classroom for Session 1 so that students have access to online sources and other materials in class.

Resources

Find it in your handbook	*The Bedford Handbook*, 8e	*A Writer's Reference*, 7e	*Rules for Writers*, 7e	*A Pocket Style Manual*, 6e
Conducting research	Conducting research (46)	Conducting research (R1)	Conducting research (53)	Finding appropriate sources (26)
Evaluating sources	Evaluating sources (47)	Evaluating sources (R2)	Evaluating sources (54)	Evaluating sources (27)
Managing information; avoiding plagiarism	Managing information; avoiding plagiarism (48)	Managing information; avoiding plagiarism (R3)	Managing information; avoiding plagiarism (55)	Avoiding plagiarism (30)
Choosing a documentation style	Choosing a documentation style (49)	Choosing a documentation style (R4)		
MLA style	Citing sources; avoiding plagiarism (51) Integrating sources (52) MLA documentation style (53)	Citing sources; avoiding plagiarism (MLA-2) Integrating sources (MLA-3) Documenting sources (MLA-4)	Citing sources; avoiding plagiarism (57) Integrating sources (58) Documenting sources (59)	Avoiding plagiarism (30) Integrating nonfiction sources (31) Integrating literary quotations (32) MLA documentation style (33)
APA style	Citing sources; avoiding plagiarism (56b) Integrating sources (56c) APA documentation style (56d)	Citing sources; avoiding plagiarism (APA-2) Integrating sources (APA-3) Documenting sources (APA-4)	Citing sources; avoiding plagiarism (62) Integrating sources (63) Documenting sources (64)	Avoiding plagiarism (36) Integrating sources (37) APA documentation style (38)
Chicago style	Citing sources; avoiding plagiarism (57b) Integrating sources (57c) *Chicago* documentation style (57d)	Citing sources; avoiding plagiarism (CMS-2) Integrating sources (CMS-3) Documenting sources (CMS-4)		Avoiding plagiarism (41) Integrating sources (42) *Chicago* documentation style (43)
CSE style				CSE documentation style (45)

Resources, *continued*

Find it in your handbook	*The Bedford Handbook*, 8e	*A Writer's Reference*, 7e	*Rules for Writers*, 7e	*A Pocket Style Manual*, 6e
Print ancillaries	*Working with Sources: Exercises for The Bedford Handbook*	*Working with Sources: Exercises for A Writer's Reference*	*Working with Sources: Exercises for Rules for Writers*	
Find it on the companion Web site	**hackerhandbooks.com/ bedhandbook**	**hackerhandbooks.com/writersref**	**hackerhandbooks.com/rules**	**hackerhandbooks.com/pocket**
Sample annotated bibliographies	Model papers > MLA Annotated Bibliography > Orlov > APA Annotated Bibliography > Haddad	Model papers > MLA Annotated Bibliography > Orlov > APA Annotated Bibliography > Haddad	Model papers > MLA Annotated Bibliography > Orlov > APA Annotated Bibliography > Haddad	Model papers > MLA Annotated Bibliography > Orlov > APA Annotated Bibliography > Haddad

Module 6
Teaching students to integrate sources and avoid plagiarism

Challenges

The academic genres that your first- and second-year students are expected to read and write may still be unfamiliar to them. While many students have had some exposure to fiction and nonfiction literature, they likely have not read researched academic essays, journal articles, and other texts written for specific, scholarly discourse communities. Because of their inexperience as both readers and writers of these types of texts, they can feel confused, ambivalent, and even frustrated when they try to use conventions of researched writing that seasoned academics employ with ease. Some of the following issues may arise when students are faced with integrating outside sources into their own texts:

- Students are not able to distinguish among quotation, summary, and paraphrase. For example, they may add quotation marks around paraphrased language.

- Students don't know how to paraphrase fairly and effectively; they think that swapping a few words out with synonyms constitutes an effective paraphrase.

- Students misidentify sources and don't provide the appropriate source details in their citations.

- Students are not familiar with signal phrases and consequently drop quotations into their papers.

- Students assume that providing a citation in a works cited or reference list allows them to add language and ideas from a source text to their own papers without in-text citations.

- Students equate plagiarism with blatant cheating and thus don't guard against unintentional plagiarism.

- Because students are unfamiliar with their handbooks, they don't understand that the handbook can help them properly identify and document various types of sources.

Strategies

Exposure to and repeated practice with sources and citations are the best strategies for helping students understand how to avoid plagiarism. To help students become more confident and accurate in their use of outside sources, focus on strategies that first expose students to models and then provide them with multiple opportunities for practice:

1. Review a variety of models, including professional journal articles and student papers, that integrate sources effectively.

2. Assign citation and plagiarism exercises from the handbook's companion Web site, as well as from ancillaries (such as *Working with Sources*).

3. In a hands-on class session, provide students with an opportunity to evaluate writing samples for effective integration of sources. The sample lesson offers step-by-step suggestions for this strategy. The lesson focuses on quotation and paraphrase. You may choose to adapt some steps for a lesson that includes summary.

Sample lesson for Strategy 3: Guided citation practice

Lesson planning:	
Sequencing:	Use this lesson before students submit the final draft of their first source-based essay. This lesson is most effective if students are writing about the same source or sources because they can better identify plagiarism if they are all familiar with the source.
Student level:	Novice writers with no experience integrating sources; intermediate writers who have some experience using sources but continue to paraphrase ineffectively. Because this lesson falls just before students submit the final draft of their first source-based essay, they will already have had some experience with college-level writing.
Learning objectives:	Students will be able to • recognize plagiarism, including the inadvertent plagiarism that results from ineffective paraphrasing • apply key skills such as using signal phrases and in-text citations, quoting and paraphrasing, and avoiding plagiarism • revise citations in their own writing to eliminate dropped quotations and plagiarism
Time required:	Three sessions of at least fifty minutes

Materials/ resources:	**Session 1** • An excerpt of a professional text, such as a journal article, that includes in-text citations in the target style (MLA, APA, or *Chicago*). Bring copies for each student, or create a transparency or an electronic copy to project. • Student drafts of their source-based essay (Each student should bring a typed copy of his or her paper.) • The handbook **Session 2** • Copies of the exercise on integrating sources and avoiding plagiarism (see p. 90) for each student • The handbook **Session 3** • Revised source-based essay drafts (Each student should bring a revised version of his or her paper.) • Highlighting pens (Ask students to bring their own.) • The handbook

Lesson steps:	

Session 1:	1. Introduce key terms and concepts that the students will need to know to integrate sources effectively. You can do this by asking students to read about these topics in the handbook for homework or by eliciting definitions and examples from more experienced class members. Introduce the following topics, pointing to the coverage of each in the handbook:
	
	  • Source text
	  • In-text citation
	  • Signal phrase/parenthetical reference
	  • Quotation
	  • Paraphrase
	  • Dropped quotation
	  • Plagiarism
	
	2. Distribute or project an excerpt of a professional text, such as a journal article, that includes in-text citations in the style you've assigned (MLA, APA, or *Chicago*).
	
	3. With help from the students, identify a few citations within the text. Draw students' attention to the parts of each citation: the signal phrase, the quotation or paraphrase, and the parenthetical reference.
	
	4. With student input, compare and contrast a paraphrase and a direct quotation. Remind students that quotations are words, phrases, or sentences taken word-for-word from the text *and* placed within quotation marks and that paraphrases are ideas from the text that writers put in their own words and sentence structure. Remind students that all language and ideas borrowed from a source should be cited.
	
	5. Spend some time reviewing the signal phrases in the professional model. Have students identify the structures, phrases, and specific words that the author uses to introduce quotations and paraphrases.

Session 1, *continued*:	6. Turn the discussion to the students' papers. Ask students to highlight quotations and paraphrases that they have added (or attempted to add) to their own texts. Ask them to check for the parts of an in-text citation: a signal phrase to introduce the text, borrowed ideas in the form of a quotation or paraphrase, and—in most cases—a parenthetical reference that includes a page number. Ask students to add any parts that are missing. (If your class is working with online sources, you will need to point out what type of information, if any, should be included in the parenthetical reference. Refer to the appropriate citation section in your handbook.)
	
	7. If time allows, ask students to exchange papers within a peer review group so that they can begin to evaluate their peers' use of signal phrases. (If your class time has run out, this step may be combined with the peer review in Session 3.) Pose questions such as the following:
	
	   • Identify a few effective signal phrases. What makes them effective?
	
	   • Are any citations misleading or incomplete or otherwise in need of improvement? If so, give your peer concrete suggestions for improving them.
	
	8. Ask students to continue revising their citations at home and to bring new, clean drafts of their papers to Session 3.

Session 2:	1. Briefly review the key concepts listed in Session 1, step 1. You can do this by brainstorming with the class or dividing students into groups to generate a list of these key terms and to describe their functions, providing examples when possible. 2. Focus students' attention on paraphrasing and plagiarism. Spend some time discussing the features of an effective paraphrase. Students often know that paraphrases should be "in their own words," but they may not be aware that the sentence structure needs to be their own as well. Point out sample effective and ineffective paraphrases from the MLA (or APA or *Chicago*) section in the handbook. Note in particular how ineffective paraphrasing can lead to inadvertent plagiarism. 3. Distribute the exercise on integrating sources and avoiding plagiarism (p. 90), and guide students through the excerpt of a source text and several student samples with integrated sources. The directions ask students to determine whether each sample attempt to integrate sources is effective (correctly quoted or paraphrased) or ineffective (plagiarized). You can discuss each student sample in the exercise one by one, first giving students an opportunity to determine an answer on their own and then discussing the correct answer with the class. Alternatively, you can divide students into groups and ask them to negotiate answers together. After about ten minutes of group time, you can discuss the correct answers with the entire class and clear up any remaining points of confusion. When completing this exercise, students may be particularly surprised at what can be considered plagiarism, such as copying an author's sentence structure too closely. Use this opportunity to reinforce the definition of plagiarism and refer students to the plagiarism policies of your course and your school. 4. If you have remaining class time, move on to the activities in Session 3. If your class time is limited, ask students to complete the remaining questions for homework. 5. Remind students to bring revised, clean drafts of their essays and their highlighting pens to the next class session.

Session 3:	1. Begin this session by briefly reviewing the qualities and components of an effectively integrated source. Ask students to contribute information about both direct quotations and paraphrases and to offer definitions of key concepts (such as *signal phrase*, *quotation*, and *paraphrase*) while you jot their responses on the board. If your students struggle, review the answers to the exercise from Session 2.
	2. Ask students to highlight all the in-text citations in their drafts. Allow them five to ten minutes to check the effectiveness of their citations and to revise them, if necessary; encourage students to refer to their handbooks and the notes on the board.
	3. After they have checked their own citations, ask students to team up to review the citations in their peers' essays. (Students can work as partners or in small groups of up to four students.) Ask students to respond to the following questions in their groups:
	• Does each citation include the necessary parts (the signal phrase, source material, and page number)?
	• Are all the citations integrated smoothly into the essay? Do signal phrases indicate what roles sources play in the draft? Are any citations particularly effective? If so, point them out. Do any need improvement? If so, give your peer concrete suggestions.
	• Is each citation accurate? Does it avoid plagiarism by fairly and accurately representing and citing the source? (Again, it's helpful if all students are working with the same source.) If not, make a concrete suggestion for improving the work.
Follow-up:	• Ask students to use the information from this lesson to revise their essays before they submit their final drafts.
	• Revisit this lesson throughout the term and assign practice exercises in your handbook or online to complete either at home or in class. Students often need repeated exposure to citation conventions to integrate sources effectively.
Variations:	• If your students will be using online sources (such as Web pages or online journal articles), point out how the in-text citations may differ. For example, students may not know how to work with unpaginated sources. Turn to your handbook's citation coverage for additional examples.
	🖥 If you are teaching online, you can ask students to find and post examples of effectively integrated sources and to explain their choices. They should note specific components of effective integration (labeling or highlighting signal phrases, parenthetical citations, and other elements, if possible) and be sure to document the source they draw on for examples. You might assign students to work in pairs, using e-mail, messaging, or a discussion space to negotiate answers. If students use an e-handbook, they can link to handbook coverage that supports their conclusions.

Resources

Find it in your handbook	*The Bedford Handbook,* 8e	*A Writer's Reference,* 7e	*Rules for Writers,* 7e	*A Pocket Style Manual,* 6e
Managing information; avoiding plagiarism	Managing information (48a and 48b) Avoiding plagiarism (48c)	Managing information; avoiding plagiarism (R3)	Managing information (55a and 55b) Avoiding plagiarism (55c)	Managing information; avoiding plagiarism (28)
Choosing a documentation style	Choosing a documentation style (49)	Choosing a documentation style (R4)		
MLA style	Citing sources (51a) Avoiding plagiarism when summarizing and paraphrasing (51b) Integrating sources (52a) Using signal phrases (52b) MLA documentation style (53)	Citing sources (MLA-2a and MLA-2b) Avoiding plagiarism when summarizing and paraphrasing (MLA-2c) Integrating sources (MLA-3a) Using signal phrases (MLA-3b) Documenting sources (MLA-4)	Citing sources; avoiding plagiarism (57) Integrating sources (58) Using signal phrases (58b) Documenting sources (59)	Avoiding plagiarism (30) Integrating nonfiction sources (31) Integrating literary quotations (32) MLA documentation style (33)
APA style	Citing sources; avoiding plagiarism (56b) Integrating sources (56c) APA documentation style (56d)	Citing sources; avoiding plagiarism (APA-2) Integrating sources (APA-3) Documenting sources (APA-4)	Citing sources; avoiding plagiarism (62) Integrating sources (63) Documenting sources (64)	Avoiding plagiarism (36) Integrating sources (37) APA documentation style (38)
Chicago style	Citing sources; avoiding plagiarism (57b) Integrating sources (57c) *Chicago* documentation style (57d)	Citing sources; avoiding plagiarism (CMS-2) Integrating sources (CMS-3) Documenting sources (CMS-4)		Avoiding plagiarism (41) Integrating sources (42) *Chicago* documentation style (43)
CSE style				CSE documentation style (45)

Resources, *continued*

Find it in your handbook	*The Bedford Handbook,* 8e	*A Writer's Reference,* 7e	*Rules for Writers,* 7e	*A Pocket Style Manual,* 6e
Print ancillaries	*Working with Sources: Exercises for The Bedford Handbook* *Research and Documentation in the Electronic Age*	*Working with Sources: Exercises for A Writer's Reference* *Research and Documentation in the Electronic Age*	*Working with Sources: Exercises for Rules for Writers* *Research and Documentation in the Electronic Age*	*Research and Documentation in the Electronic Age*
Find it on the companion Web site	**hackerhandbooks.com/ bedhandbook**	**hackerhandbooks.com/writersref**	**hackerhandbooks.com/rules**	**hackerhandbooks.com/pocket**
Online exercises	Research exercises > MLA > 50–1 to 53–8 > APA > 56–3 to 56–19 > *Chicago* > 57–3 to 57–19	MLA > MLA 2–1 to MLA 4–8 APA > APA 2–1 to APA 4–8 CMS > CMS 2–1 to CMS 4–8	MLA > 57–1 to 59–8 APA > 62–1 to 64–8	MLA > 30–1 to 33–8 APA > 36–1 to 38–8 *Chicago* > 41–1 to 43–8
Other online resources	*Research and Documentation Online* (includes model papers) Tutorials > *Paraphrase and summary* (MLA)* > *Integrating sources* (MLA)*	*Research and Documentation Online* (includes model papers) Tutorials > *Paraphrase and summary* (MLA)* > *Integrating sources* (MLA)*	*Research and Documentation Online* (includes model papers) Tutorials > *Paraphrase and summary* (MLA)* > *Integrating sources* (MLA)*	*Research and Documentation Online* (includes model papers)

* Premium resources: As a registered instructor, you have access to all free and all premium resources for your handbook. Your students will have access if their books are packaged with activation codes or if they purchase access online.

Exercise on integrating sources and avoiding plagiarism (MLA style)

Read the following passage and the information about its source. Then decide whether each student sample uses the source correctly. If the student has made an error in quoting, paraphrasing, or citing the source, revise the sample to avoid the error. If the student has used the source correctly, write "OK." Identify pages in the handbook that help you determine whether the source is correctly integrated.

ORIGINAL SOURCE

There are 385 units of the National Park System of the United States, and it is likely that some portion of every one is the result of private philanthropy. Whether the nucleus of an entire national park (as at Virgin Islands National Park on St. John) or the contents of a major interpretive center (as at Pecos National Historical Park) were a gift to the nation by a private individual or individuals, the art of giving to create or expand the parks, and through them benefit the American people and American wildlife, was well developed and widely practiced until World War II. This is not so much the case now, and one wonders why. It may also be that there is a resurgent interest in wildlands philanthropy these days, though largely from foundations rather than individuals. While public support and funding for protection of natural areas will continue to be fundamental, private conservation efforts are a necessary complement; without philanthropy, the national parks will not thrive.

The general public tends to believe that national parks consist of lands purchased by the United States government in places where a federal agency—the National Park Service—set out consciously to preserve a landscape, to protect a natural resource, to commemorate a historical event. This is far from the truth, even though some parks have been created in just this way. Parks are the product of a political process, and that process often gets its start from the dream of one person, or a small group of people, who put their minds, their energies, their time, and often their money into making a park happen.

From Winks, Robin W. "Philanthropy and National Parks." *Wild Earth: Wild Ideas for a World Out of Balance*. Ed. Tom Butler. Minneapolis: Milkweed, 2002. Print. The source passage is from pages 70–71.

Student samples with integrated source material

1.   Winks points out that the National Park System received most of its land before the Second World War, when private donations were common. "This is not so much the case now, and one wonders why" (70).

2.   Winks acknowledges that although the donation of land from individuals to the National Park System is no longer typical, the preservation of wild areas by organizations is common (70).

3.   According to Winks, private conservation efforts are just as important as public support and funding dedicated to protecting natural areas (70).

4.   Winks notes that without philanthropy, the national parks will not thrive (70).

5.   "Parks are the product of a political process," Winks writes, "and that process often gets its start from the dream of one person, or a small group of people" who dedicate themselves to "making a park happen" (70).

Answer key: Sample student attempts to integrate the source

1. **Incorrect.** The second sentence is a dropped quotation; it does not have a signal phrase. Refer students to the chart "Using signal phrases in MLA papers" in the MLA section of your handbook.

   Possible revision: Winks points out that the National Park System received most of its land before the Second World War, when private donations were common. "This is not so much the case now," he laments, "and one wonders why" (70).

2. **Correct.** This is an effective paraphrase. The sentence maintains the idea of the original source without using any unique language or sentence structure from the source.

3. **Incorrect.** This is an ineffective paraphrase, and it is unintentional plagiarism. The sentence includes several phrases that are lifted directly from the source (*private conservation efforts*, *public support and funding*, and *protect*[*ing*] . . . *natural areas*). Students should refer to the MLA section of the handbook that deals with paraphrases.

   Possible revision: Winks argues that public funding alone cannot save national parks. Individual support is key to the survival and growth of protected lands.

4. **Incorrect.** This sentence is plagiarized even though the writer gives the author's name and a page number. Except for the signal phrase, the sentence is lifted word-for-word from the source. Refer students to the MLA section of the handbook that deals with enclosing borrowed language in quotation marks.

   Possible revision: Winks notes that "without philanthropy, the national parks will not thrive" (70).

5. **Correct.** This is an effective quotation, properly cited. The sentence places all wording from the source within quotation marks.

Module 7
Teaching grammar and punctuation

Challenges

When you assess the first batch of papers for a given class, you'll likely discover that not all students know how to edit their work effectively for an academic audience. Specifically, one or more of the following issues might surface:

- Students use spoken, regional, or cultural varieties of English where academic (standard) forms are expected.

- Students rely on their *sense* of what is correct rather than on a formal understanding of English sentence structure.

- While students understand grammar instruction and can recognize forms in sample sentences, they still have difficulty applying the rules in their own writing.

- Students don't use the handbook or other reference tools as they write; they instead expect the instructor to correct grammar and punctuation errors for them.

- Not all students have the same needs, so instructors may have a difficult time designing activities that can be adapted to the students' varying skill levels.

Strategies

To help students learn to edit effectively, use strategies such as the following that heighten their understanding of standard English patterns and require them to revisit their own writing:

1. Use grammar and punctuation exercises, such as those in the handbook (if available) or on the companion Web site, as a first step in teaching a pattern.

> **In this module:**
>
> Challenges 93
>
> Strategies 93
> - *Sample lesson for Strategy 3 94*
>
> Resources 98
> - *Editing log 99*

2. Require students to correct errors you have identified on drafts before they submit their final papers.

3. Require students to maintain editing logs (lists of their own errors with examples and with corrections). The sample lesson provides specific guidelines for applying this strategy.

Sample lesson for Strategy 3: Using an editing log

Lesson planning:	
Sequencing:	Prepare for this lesson from the beginning of the term; use this lesson after one or more essays have been assessed and returned to students.
Student level:	Novice to advanced; any students who have one or more grammar or punctuation errors in their work
Learning objectives:	Students will be able to • correct grammar and punctuation mistakes in their work • identify or explain the rule or pattern used to correct their errors
Time required:	One session of at least fifty minutes to introduce and begin the log
Materials/ resources:	• The handbook • Completed essays or drafts with errors that you have identified but not corrected • Paper for each student (Ask students to bring their own notebook paper.) Optional: • A copy of the editing log for each student (See p. 99.) • An electronic copy or a transparency of the editing log and a projector

→

Lesson steps:	
Preparation:	1. From the beginning of the term, introduce students to grammar and punctuation rules in mini-lessons or homework assignments. A simple way to preview grammar topics is to ask students to read the appropriate pages in the handbook, complete the related exercises for homework, and review some or all of the answers in class. Focus on those errors that occur most frequently or that seem to cause the most confusion for your students. (Comma splices, fragments, and missing commas after introductory elements are common errors and thus are good topics to begin with.)
	2. When you assess students' papers during the term, identify grammar and punctuation problems by circling, highlighting, underlining, or placing a check mark next to errors. Alternatively, you can code each error with a handbook section number. Do not correct the errors; simply point them out. *For examples of comments on student papers, see Topic 3.*
	When you mark errors, you can choose to identify only those related to grammar topics you have already covered in class, or you can identify any errors that are addressed in the handbook. Use your judgment to determine which method will best suit your students' needs and abilities.
	How many errors you mark also depends on your assessment of your students' needs. For example, you might mark only the errors in one paragraph, only the errors on one page, or only the first ten errors in the paper. Choose a number that is manageable for both you and your students. *See "Managing the paper load" in Topic 3.*
	3. When you return papers to students, alert them that they will need to use your feedback to complete their editing logs. Remind them to keep their papers in a safe place, preferably a folder or binder designated just for your class. Ask them to bring these papers to class on the day you plan to introduce the log.
Session 1:	1. Explain to students the rationale of revisiting their own work to edit mistakes. • Explain that while there are many varieties of English, students are expected to use academic (standard written) English in most college classes and professional settings. • Acknowledge that not everyone speaks standard English all the time (in fact, very few people do), so their own usage might contain a few patterns that are considered "errors" in standard English. • Acknowledge that although exercises are a starting point, students can become good editors only by continuing to polish their own work.

2. Introduce the class to the format of the editing log by projecting a sample grid or sketching it on the board.

Original sentence:
Edited sentence:
Rule or pattern applied:

3. Hand out an editing log page to each student, or ask students to copy the grid onto their own paper.

4. Using some examples that the students volunteer, play the part of the student and model the process of completing an entry in the log:

   • Look over the feedback on an essay and find a sentence that contains an error.

   • Copy the original sentence to the log. Circle, underline, highlight, or in some way mark the error in the original sentence.

   • Using your handbook as necessary, write an edited version of the sentence below the original. Circle, underline, highlight, or in some way mark the correction in the edited sentence.

   • Write the grammar rule or pattern from the handbook that you used to edit the error. Rather than describing the error (such as "missing comma"), explain how to fix the mistake ("add a comma after an introductory element").

Sample

Original sentence: Air pollution poses risks to all <u>humans it</u> can be deadly for asthma sufferers.
Edited sentence: Air pollution poses risks to all humans<u>, but</u> it can be deadly for asthma sufferers.
Rule or pattern applied: To edit a run-on sentence, use a comma and a coordinating conjunction (*and, but, or*). (Handbook section 20)

Session 1, *continued*:	5. Encourage students to begin their own logs in class. Allow time for students to complete at least two entries so that they can address concerns or seek help from you.
Follow-up:	• Collect the editing logs periodically or at the midpoint and end of the term to assign credit for the work completed. Provide students with additional feedback if necessary. • Encourage students to refer to their logs during the editing stage of any essay project so that they can find and correct similar mistakes.
Variations:	• Assign the editing log as a take-home quiz after each essay is returned or as a midterm exam after two or more essays have been returned. If some students have few or no errors to correct, you can assign automatic credit for these quizzes as a reward for their effort. • Require the editing log as part of a writing portfolio. Ask students to write a reflection or cover letter for the log explaining how their editing skills have improved during the semester. 💻 If you are teaching online, introduce students to the editing log with the tools you use to present other lectures or lessons. When you assess students' papers, use the highlight, underline, or font color function in your word processing program to identify errors in students' work.

Resources

Find it in your handbook	*The Bedford Handbook*, 8e	*A Writer's Reference*, 7e	*Rules for Writers*, 7e	*A Pocket Style Manual*, 6e
Revising and editing	Revise and edit sentences; proofread the final draft (2b)	Revise and edit sentences (C3-b)	Revise and edit sentences; proofread the final draft (3b and 3c)	
Grammar topics	Clear Sentences (8 to 15) Word Choice (16 to 18) Grammatical Sentences (19 to 27) Challenges for ESL and Multilingual Writers (28 to 31)	Sentence Style (S1 to S7) Word Choice (W1 to W6) Grammatical Sentences (G1 to G6) Multilingual Writers and ESL Challenges (M1 to M5)	Clarity (8 to 18) Grammar (19 to 27) ESL Challenges (28 to 31)	Clarity (1 to 9) Grammar (10 to 16)
Punctuation and mechanics	Punctuation (32 to 39) Mechanics (40 to 45)	Punctuation and Mechanics (P1 to P10)	Punctuation (32 to 39) Mechanics (40 to 45)	Punctuation (17 to 21) Mechanics (22 to 24)
Print ancillaries	*Resources for Multilingual Writers and ESL*, a Hacker Handbooks Supplement	*Resources for Multilingual Writers and ESL*, a Hacker Handbooks Supplement *Exercises for A Writer's Reference*	*Resources for Multilingual Writers and ESL*, a Hacker Handbooks Supplement	*Resources for Multilingual Writers and ESL*, a Hacker Handbooks Supplement
Find it on the companion Web site	**hackerhandbooks.com/ bedhandbook**	**hackerhandbooks.com/writersref**	**hackerhandbooks.com/rules**	**hackerhandbooks.com/pocket**
Online exercises	Grammar exercises	Grammar exercises	Grammar exercises	Grammar exercises

Editing log

Original sentence:

Edited sentence:

Rule or pattern applied:

Original sentence:

Edited sentence:

Rule or pattern applied:

Original sentence:

Edited sentence:

Rule or pattern applied:

Module 8
Teaching with peer review

Challenges

When orchestrated effectively, peer review can provide students with critical feedback and an authentic collaborative writing experience before their final drafts are completed. If, however, students don't trust the process or don't feel that they have adequate preparation, they may see peer review as a fruitless exercise. Some specific challenges you might encounter include the following:

- Students don't take the process seriously. They think that the instructor's opinion is the only one that counts and don't value the feedback of their peers.

- Students resist constructively criticizing their peers' work because they don't want to hurt feelings.

- Students don't feel that their knowledge of writing or grammar qualifies them to critique another student's work.

- Students are not invested in the process and therefore provide only vague responses.

- Students think of peer review as editing; they attempt to correct surface errors and neglect global issues.

- Students don't understand that responding to writing in a peer review can help them become better critical readers.

Strategies

Make peer review more effective for students by building their trust in the process and giving them an opportunity to show their strengths and opinions as readers rather than editors. You can do so by using the following strategies:

1. Work with students to develop guidelines and a rubric for evaluating the quality of feedback that reviewers provide.

2. Provide clear guidelines to avoid turning peer review sessions into editing workshops. Ask students to focus their comments on the effectiveness of the paper's argument, organization, or support, for example, rather than on punctuation or grammar.

3. Model the types of questions that good reviewers ask throughout the peer review process: for example, "What is the writer's main idea?" and "Does the paper have enough appropriate support for the thesis?"

4. Train students to provide effective feedback using sample papers. Model the peer review process for the class. The sample lesson offers step-by-step suggestions for using this strategy.

Sample lesson for Strategy 4: Guided peer review

Lesson planning:	
Sequencing:	Use this lesson during the drafting stage of any writing assignment, preferably early in the term.
Student level:	Both novice and experienced writers
Learning objectives:	Students will be able to • identify the features of a high-quality peer review session • effectively review a peer's work by pointing out strengths, areas in need of improvement, or both
Time required:	Two sessions of at least fifty minutes
Materials/ resources:	• For Session 1, at least three sample papers to review. The papers can be models that you have written or anonymous student papers from previous terms. For this guided review, it's best if the papers are brief—between 500 and 750 words. (To save paper, produce a photocopy for every two or three students, and collect the sample papers at the end of the period to use with other sections of your class. Students should be able to read the samples without straining, but they don't need individual copies.) • For Session 2, one sample paper for the whole class to review, and students' own essay drafts for peer review in groups
Lesson steps:	
Session 1:	1. Open class by discussing the rationale for using peer review, covering any or all of the following ideas: • Writing does not take place in a vacuum. • Meaning is created when readers engage with a piece of writing. • A peer's feedback provides perspectives that the author might not consider when working alone. • All professional writing is to some extent collaborative.

→

Lesson steps:	
Session 1, *continued*:	2. Give students an opportunity to share what they found most and least valuable about their past peer review experiences. As they offer their ideas, jot their responses on the board. 3. Encouraging students to draw from the ideas on the board, work together as a class to develop a set of guidelines for high-quality peer reviews. Remind students that they can avoid negative experiences with peer review by clearly asserting their expectations at this point. Students will most likely need specific direction in this step to think of peer review as more than proofreading. Guide them to consider all the salient features of a paper that peers can comment on, including the thesis, organization, style, voice, and support. **Sample peer review guidelines** A high-quality peer review - comments on the effectiveness of the thesis - describes at least two specific strengths in the paper - offers one specific suggestion for improvement 4. Distribute copies of the first sample paper or project it on the board. (Remember, to save paper, you don't need to provide a separate copy for each student.) Work with students to conduct a review that adheres to all of the students' guidelines for a high-quality peer review. Students often see the flaws in other works and tend to ignore the strengths. In this step, encourage them to provide well-rounded feedback. 5. Revisit the guidelines the class has established, and ask students to reflect on their role as reviewers. Did the guidelines feel restrictive? Did reviewers withhold comments that they felt might have been helpful? Or were students uncomfortable providing some of the feedback the guidelines required? Allow the students to suggest revisions to the guidelines if necessary, and record their suggestions. 6. After class, type up the peer review guidelines that your class has created. Make photocopies or prepare an electronic copy to distribute or post online and to project in class. **Note:** To ensure that your students can comment on the models with confidence, you may want to spend more time modeling the process and working through sample papers as a class. Many students begin to feel comfortable after two or three sample reviews, though you can, of course, revisit these steps as many times and at as many points in the semester as needed.

Session 2:	1. Warm up by reviewing a sample paper with the whole class. Distribute or project the guidelines that your class developed during Session 1. Allow students to ask questions about the sample paper, guidelines, or peer review process in general.
	2. Divide students into groups of three or four. You can divide them up in a number of ways: alphabetically by first or last name, by birth month or season, by counting off in threes or fours, or any other similar method.
	3. Ask students to pass their papers clockwise or counterclockwise within each group and begin to read *without* pens in hand.
	Students will be tempted to mark on their peers' papers, but encourage them to read without marking so that they avoid simply proofreading the paper. If they would like to write, ask them to take notes on separate sheets of paper, not on the peer's work.
	Ask students to continue reading and passing the papers for an amount of time that you determine. (Students will need more time if reviewing longer papers. Choose an amount of time that fits the assignment and your class period. If students are working on a very long paper, consider asking them to exchange with only one peer, not several.)
	4. After the reading period, encourage students to discuss each paper with their group, sticking to the guidelines the class has established for reviewers.
	Early in the semester, while students are just getting to know one another, you can ask them to focus only on the strengths of the papers they review. As they begin to feel more comfortable with one another, you can ask them to also look at areas in need of improvement. During the discussion period, each writer should feel free to ask questions of the reviewers and take notes or make corrections on his or her own paper.
	Encourage students to be active in this process. You may need to visit each group to provide additional modeling until the students feel comfortable.
	5. Near the end of the session, give students a few minutes to begin revising on their own. They may want to start making changes to their work while the ideas and suggestions are still fresh.
	6. Optional: At the end of the class period or at the beginning of the next class, ask students to rate the quality of their peers' reviews. They can use symbols—such as a plus (+), check mark (✓), and minus (–)—or single words—such as *thorough*, *average*, and *vague*—to denote the grade categories. Take these ratings into consideration as you calculate the students' participation grades at the end of the term.
Follow-up:	• Ask students to revise their drafts using the comments from the peer review sessions. Remind your students that they don't have to take their peers' advice if they have a clear reason for rejecting it; the comments of peers are suggestions, not commands. You might ask students to write about their application or rejection of their peers' suggestions and to submit those comments with their revised paper.
	• Conduct additional peer review sessions for new drafts of the same assignment or for future assignments. Students' reviewing abilities will grow with each opportunity to practice the process.
	• Model the peer review process several times during the term. (See the final note in Session 1.)

Variations:	• Create guidelines for different purposes: reviewing thesis statements, reviewing organization, reviewing citations, and so forth.
	• If the assignment has very specific instructions, such as a requirement for a certain number of outside sources, draw up those guidelines ahead of time and develop further guidelines with the class.
	If you are working in an online platform, consider using the discussion board for peer reviews. Students can follow the guidelines that the class establishes for excellent reviews.

Resources

Find it in your handbook	*The Bedford Handbook*, 8e	*A Writer's Reference*, 7e	*Rules for Writers*, 7e	*A Pocket Style Manual*, 6e
Revision	Approach global revisions in cycles (2a) Revising sentences (2b)	Make global revisions (C3-a) Revise and edit sentences (C3-b)	Make global revisions (3a) Revising sentences (3b)	
Peer review	Guidelines for peer reviewers (p. 38) Checklist for global revision (p. 40)	Checklist for global revision (p. 21)	Checklist for global revision (p. 36)	Checklist for global revision (endpapers)
Find it on the companion Web site	**hackerhandbooks .com/ bedhandbook**	**hackerhandbooks .com/writersref**	**hackerhandbooks .com/rules**	**hackerhandbooks .com/pocket**
Online exercises	Writing exercises > 2–1	Writing exercises > C3–1	The Writing Process > 3–1	
Other online resources	Tutorials > *Revising with peer comments**	Tutorials > *Revising with peer comments**	Tutorials > *Revising with peer comments**	

* Premium resources: As a registered instructor, you have access to all free and all premium resources for your handbook. Your students will have access if their books are packaged with activation codes or if they purchase access online.

Module 9
Teaching visual literacy

by Elizabeth Canfield

Challenges

The use of visuals as popular communication has greatly increased as various media have become more accessible in digital formats. In addition to encountering visuals such as ads and photographs in traditional print media, students are constantly bombarded by the visuals they find online, such as Web pages and YouTube videos. However comfortable they may feel with visual media, they may not understand how to think critically about images or how to analyze them in an essay.

Incorporating analysis of visual images into your course may present some of the following challenges:

- Students resist the idea that visuals are anything more than entertainment.

- Students used to accessing, creating, or manipulating visual files assume that they know all they need to about visuals. They have difficulty, however, identifying the rhetorical components of a visual image.

- Although students might be able to describe visuals, they don't recognize that visuals, like written texts, can be subjects of analysis.

- Without a rhetorical context, students don't see how a discussion of visual media is related to writing or critical thinking.

- Although students might have analyzed visuals previously, they don't know how to communicate their understanding of visual rhetoric in an essay.

Strategies

Some of the following strategies may help you provide practice and guidance for students learning to analyze and write about visuals:

1. Provide models of analysis of visual images, both in writing and through class discussion.

2. So that students recognize the importance of understanding visuals that influence them every day, subjects for analysis should be common and familiar (related to popular culture or current events, for example).

3. Draw connections between analysis of written texts and analysis of visual images; talk about visuals as texts that can be read. Show students examples of words and visuals working together to make meaning.

4. Discuss how visuals can present arguments. See the sample lesson for this strategy.

Sample lesson for Strategy 4: Discussing visual arguments

Lesson planning:	
Sequencing:	Use this lesson at any point in the semester. Often, teaching analysis of visual images goes hand in hand with teaching argument and argument analysis.
Student level:	This lesson is designed for students who have little experience with analysis of visual images but are familiar with written arguments.
Learning objectives:	Students will be able to • describe the basic design elements of a visual • write a draft rhetorical analysis of a visual
Time required:	Two sessions of at least fifty minutes
Materials/ resources:	• A common but effective visual image, either projected on the screen or made into a handout for students • The handbook (for reference during discussion and workshop) • Optional: A handout (projected or printed) that outlines the questions for Session 1

Lesson steps:	
Session 1:	1. Share the image that you are using for analysis.
	2. Using the following questions, conduct a think-pair-share exercise in which students come up with their own answers and maybe do some freewriting before discussing their thoughts with a partner. The pair will then present the results of their discussion to the class. (The following questions are intended to elicit gut reactions and observations. In this step, students should not attempt interpretation or evaluation of purpose or audience.)
	• When you first looked at this image, what did you think about? What was your first reaction?
	• What is the original medium of the image (photograph, painting, and so on)? How can you tell?
	• What is the subject of the image?
	• How would you describe the composition of the image? What shapes, angles, colors, or other elements do you notice? What is in the foreground? What is in the background?
	• What perspective (point of view) does the image present? From what vantage point does the eye appear to be viewing the image (head-on or from high up, for example)?
	• Are any words mixed with the image? If so, how prominent are they? What message do they convey?
	3. After students have thought through these questions on their own and shared with a partner, ask pairs to present their ideas to the class. As students share with the larger group, take notes on the board or project them. Once all the students have shared their ideas, ask them to look over your notes and make observations about what they found. What responses did students have in common? Did the class seem divided on any points?
	4. Deepening the discussion: Bring students back to the think-pair-share format with the following questions. Remind students to support their answers with details from the visual.
	• What is the purpose of this image? What is this image supposed to *do*?
	• Who do you think is the target audience for this image? What makes you think that?
	• Earlier, you made some comments about the composition of the image (its elements and structure). *Why* do you think it is composed in this way? How does the composition of the image help convey and enhance its meaning?
	• We've already talked about the presence of words with the image. How do words change or enhance the meaning of the visual?
	• Does the image (along with any accompanying words) make an argument? Support your answer with specific details.
	5. Again, as student pairs share with the larger group, take notes. Once every pair has spoken, talk about points on which the class agrees and points on which it is split. Ask pairs to further defend their conclusions when interpretations differ.

Session 1, *continued*:	6. To prepare the class for Session 2, ask students to write a two-page essay that analyzes the image as a visual text. They should begin the essay with an introduction that briefly describes the visual image (a summary) and include a thesis about the meaning of the visual. Body paragraphs should explore how the visual's composition contributes to its overall meaning. Students should draw on the class discussion when supporting their interpretation with evidence. *For a sample essay assignment, see Assignment 5 in Part III.*
Session 2:	1. Have students critically discuss their papers with a partner. To focus their conversations, provide questions such as the following: • Take a moment to read the essay. What is the thesis? • How does the writer structure the essay to support that thesis? What evidence does the writer present? Is the thesis well supported? If not, provide specific suggestions for revision. • Who is the audience for the writer's essay? How can you tell? • What has the writer left out of the essay that needs to be added? • Likewise, what details or discussions are extraneous? What should be streamlined or omitted? 2. During the last few minutes of class or for homework, ask students to reflect in writing on the process of analyzing a visual text. How did writing about the visual deepen their understanding of its meaning? Did writing about the visual reveal something that the class discussion did not? How might this exercise in examining visual texts be relevant for future analyses of written (verbal) texts?
Follow-up:	If you require that students incorporate visuals into an essay of their own, have them bring their visuals in for brief class discussions based on the questions in Session 1. If topics vary, have students describe the context in which their visuals will appear. As much as possible, help students make connections between analyzing and integrating visual sources and written sources.
Variations:	• Session 1 of this module can stand alone. • Students can create their own visual arguments for group or class analysis using the questions in Session 1. • If you are teaching online, you can post the visual to a class discussion board or blog, where the entire class can comment individually. For Session 2, students can be placed in small virtual discussion groups for reading and commenting on one another's written responses to the visual. An online discussion allows students to post multimedia examples in their responses.

Resources

Find it in your handbook	*The Bedford Handbook*, 8e	*A Writer's Reference*, 7e	*Rules for Writers*, 7e	*A Pocket Style Manual*, 6e
Analyzing visual texts	Writing about texts (4)	Writing about texts (A1)	Writing about texts (5)	
Using visuals	Add visuals to support your purpose (58d)	Add visuals to supplement your text (C5-d)	Add visuals to supplement your text (50d)	
Print ancillaries	*Designing Documents and Understanding Visuals*, a Hacker Handbooks Supplement	*Designing Documents and Understanding Visuals*, a Hacker Handbooks Supplement	*Designing Documents and Understanding Visuals*, a Hacker Handbooks Supplement	*Designing Documents and Understanding Visuals*, a Hacker Handbooks Supplement

Module 10
Addressing writing in the disciplines

by Terry Myers Zawacki

Challenges

Students traveling from course to course across the curriculum encounter such a wide variety of writing assignments and teacher expectations that they may not understand how writing skills transfer from one setting to another. They may need you to clarify the relevance of your assignments for writing tasks in other courses. Varying expectations and grading policies can make even the most competent writers question their ability to write well in college. As a writing teacher, you may face some of the following related challenges:

- Students lack confidence as writers because they don't understand why they encounter varying assignments and expectations in different courses.

- Teachers and students alike sometimes assume that "good" academic writing means the same thing from one teacher and course to the next across the curriculum, even though formats, conventions, and individual teacher preferences may differ.

- Students become frustrated when they find out that genres with the same name (a book review, for example) may carry different meanings, depending on the course and the discipline.

- Students don't understand how the writing and rhetorical skills they learn in a composition class can be applied to writing assignments in other academic contexts.

- Students are unaccustomed to reflecting on their own writing and have trouble adapting their writing to suit courses and teachers across disciplines.

Strategies

Working with the following strategies can help your students recognize the foundation elements of strong academic writing and understand the roots and value of varying requirements and expectations across disciplines.

For specific instructor and student self-reflection prompts, see "Helping students become rhetorically aware writers" in Topic 5.

1. Think about your academic writing experiences and practices and model self-reflection for students. Give students opportunities to reflect on their own experiences and practices as writers.

2. Discuss with students your goals and expectations for them as writers. Explain how these goals and expectations are related to your academic background and the requirements of your department and school.

3. Introduce students to rhetorical features that are common to academic writing across disciplines (reasoned analysis and claims supported by evidence, for example) and those that are discipline specific (such as conventions for genres, formatting, use of evidence, and structure and style).

4. Work with students to examine assignments they receive in other courses. Help students analyze varying expectations in courses across the curriculum.

5. Help students analyze one of your assignments, including your goals and expectations for them as writers, the context those goals and expectations reflect, the genre and rhetorical strategies you are asking students to practice, and the rhetorical knowledge that will transfer to other courses across the curriculum. Ask students to suggest ways that you can clarify your goals and expectations. The sample lesson provides specific guidelines for applying this strategy.

Sample lesson for Strategy 5: Analyzing an assignment

Lesson planning:	
Sequencing:	Use this lesson when you hand out the first major writing assignment. You may want to use variations of this lesson for subsequent assignments you give and for assignments students encounter in other courses.
Student level:	This activity will work best if students can draw on previous writing assignments in other disciplines. Late high school or early college writing experience is sufficient.
Learning objectives:	Students will be able to • identify and draw on what they know about genres and rhetorical strategies to help them understand writing assignments • recognize the contexts for their teachers' assignments and expectations • identify similarities and differences between your assignments and expectations and those of other teachers in your discipline and other disciplines • identify conventions of academic writing that cut across disciplines and those that are specific to particular disciplines

Time required:	Two sessions of at least fifty minutes; some outside preparation
Materials/ resources:	• Blackboard or computer and projector (or overhead projector with transparencies) • Copies of essay assignment and chart (see p. 119)

Lesson steps:

Preparation for Session 1:	For homework, give students a draft of your first essay assignment prompt and ask them to write in response to the following set of prompts (you may find it useful to review the assignment prompt yourself and write out your own responses):
	• Think about the papers you've written for your courses in college or in the last two years of high school. Make a list of the kinds of papers you were asked to write. Include the name of the course for which you completed each assignment.
	• Turn to the writing assignment you've been given for this course. Based on the name of the assignment (such as essay, argument, analysis, narrative), describe the kind of writing you think is expected. What features (tone, support, format, for example) do you associate with this type of writing? Are those associations based on assignments of the same category from other courses you've taken? Which courses?
	• Read and annotate the prompt. Underline the key words in the assignment that help you understand the writing task, the form and structure you should use (for example, whether you need a thesis and where it should be placed or whether to use headings and subheadings), what kind of information to include and how much, how formal or informal you should sound, and so on.
	• Consider whether this assignment is similar to or different from the kinds of papers you've written in other courses. Does this assignment seem to be typical of a particular type of course (literature, history, or creative writing, for example)? Or does the paper you're being asked to write seem to be different in almost every way from papers you've written in other classes? Be sure to explain your response.
	• Why do you think you have been given this writing assignment? As far as you can tell from the description, what are the teacher's goals and expectations? How do you know? Are some things not spelled out but rather written "between the lines"? If so, what is implied rather than explicitly stated?
	• What standards or criteria will be applied in the evaluation of this assignment? Which of them are similar to those that other teachers have applied, and which are different?
Session 1:	1. Begin by making sure students understand the terms *discipline*, *genre*, and *rhetorical strategy*. You can use their responses to the prep work to illustrate each of these terms.
	2. In class, explain to students that the names teachers give to the types of writing they assign (genres such as argument essay or lab report) often reflect preferences and conventions specific to their discipline. Key words in the assignment (*narration*, *description*, and *contrast*, for example) specify the rhetorical strategies to be used in responding to the assignment prompt. (To provide a concrete example, you can ask students when they might use narration. Their answers might include *personal essays*, *autobiographies*, *case studies*, or *crime reports*.)

Session 1, *continued*:	3. Put students into groups of four to share and expand the ideas they began forming with their homework responses. One student in each group should take notes. To keep the discussion focused, provide specific guidelines:

3. Put students into groups of four to share and expand the ideas they began forming with their homework responses. One student in each group should take notes. To keep the discussion focused, provide specific guidelines:

- Ask students to list the names teachers have given to the papers they've assigned. They should consider how assignments of the same name have differed from one teacher or course to the next (for example, how an "essay" they've written for an English course might be different from an essay they've written for a history course).

- Ask students to discuss and note the rhetorical, structural, and textual features they associate with the genres they've listed.

  They can consider, for example, how different genres might use narration or description or the kinds of things they've been asked to compare and contrast for different courses.

  They can discuss the different ways teachers have expected them to structure their papers and differences they've noticed in teachers' preferences for textual features such as introductions, the placement of a thesis sentence, the use of headings and subheadings, using and citing sources, and stylistic features such as length of paragraphs and sentences, use of figurative language, and so on.

- Ask the groups to fill in a chart (see p. 119 for a sample) listing the genres they've discussed, their rhetorical and/or disciplinary purposes, and the structures and other textual features that seem to be most typical of each. They should note which genres and textual features seem to apply across disciplines and which seem to be particular to courses in specific disciplines. (If you teach in a networked classroom or an online space, provide this chart electronically so that groups can share their work. If not, provide each group with a transparency of the chart.)

- Finally, ask the groups to turn their attention back to your assignment and to discuss the genre knowledge they will draw on to respond to the assignment. Ask them to make a list of the key words and descriptions they've used as cues to figure out your expectations.

4. Ask students to present the results of their group's discussion to the class. Give each group no more than fifteen minutes to present, as there will no doubt be considerable overlap. (Consider asking each group if they can think of another, more effective way of conveying this information, such as a diagram or list. Explain to them that writers should always make decisions about appropriate genres, formats, structures, and conventions based on the rhetorical situation—that is, the purpose, the audience, and the task.)

5. At the end of the class, ask students to do a little reflective writing on their own. They should write a few paragraphs about how this analysis has changed their understanding of expectations for academic writing in general and the features of writing that are specific to disciplines. What writing skills and genre knowledge can they apply to your assignment that they might also apply to assignments in other courses and disciplines?

Note: This reflective writing can occur in the last ten minutes of class, after class in a journal, online on a class discussion board, or in an informal homework assignment to be turned in for the next class. You might choose not to collect this writing.

Session 2:	1. In a large group discussion, ask students what questions they still have about how to accomplish your assignment successfully. Do students understand the goals and requirements of the assignment? Are any guidelines missing or vague? Are objectives clearly stated? 2. Following this discussion, ask students to work together to make revisions to the assignment, clarifying the language, refining or adding guidelines or objectives, or inserting more detailed explanations. Encourage them to draft anything they feel is missing. They should provide concrete solutions for any problems. (As an incentive, you may decide to give extra credit or points to the groups whose revisions become part of the final version of your assignment.)
Follow-up:	• To extend the benefits of this assignment, you may want to ask students to bring in copies of assignments from other courses and work through a similar set of prompts. Call on volunteers to explain how their assignments fit into the course, what the teacher seems to expect, and the contexts (general academic, disciplinary, institutional, and personal) for the teacher's expectations. Working from a few such assignments, the class can list the key terms teachers use to describe assignments, as well as the formats, structures, kinds of evidence, and stylistic conventions they expect. • To encourage further reflection on this activity, you might ask students to write a letter of advice to first-year students about how to successfully respond to assignments and meet expectations across disciplines. • Reflection on learning helps students transfer knowledge and skills from one context to another. Give your students frequent opportunities to reflect on what they have learned in your course about academic writing and themselves as academic writers and on what skills and abilities they still need to learn to become confident, flexible writers capable of meeting expectations across the curriculum.

Resources

Find it in your handbook	*The Bedford Handbook,* 8e	*A Writer's Reference,* 7e	*Rules for Writers,* 7e	*A Pocket Style Manual,* 6e
Writing in the disciplines	Writing in the disciplines (7)	Writing in the disciplines (A4)		
MLA style	Writing MLA papers (50 to 55)	MLA papers (MLA-1 to MLA-5)	Writing MLA papers (56 to 60)	
APA style	Writing APA papers (56)	APA papers (APA-1 to APA-5)	Writing APA papers (61 to 65)	
Chicago style	Writing *Chicago* papers (57)	*Chicago* papers (CMS-1 to CMS-5)		
Print ancillaries	*Writing in the Disciplines: Advice and Models,* a Hacker Handbooks Supplement	*Writing in the Disciplines: Advice and Models,* a Hacker Handbooks Supplement	*Writing in the Disciplines: Advice and Models,* a Hacker Handbooks Supplement	*Writing in the Disciplines: Advice and Models,* a Hacker Handbooks Supplement
Find it on the companion Web site	**hackerhandbooks .com/ bedhandbook**	**hackerhandbooks .com/writersref**	**hackerhandbooks .com/rules**	**hackerhandbooks .com/pocket**
Research and documentation	*Research and Documentation Online*	*Research and Documentation Online*	*Research and Documentation Online*	*Research and Documentation Online*

Sample chart for lesson on writing in the disciplines, Session 1 (See p. 115.)

Type of writing assignment (genre)	Course/discipline	Task, purpose, and rhetorical strategies	Kinds of evidence required	Most prominent textual features called for	Other teacher directives and advice
Personal essay	Composition	Describe a turning point in your life. Narrate the event with lots of specific description.	Personal experience	First person; chronological order; vivid details; dialogue and other story devices	Craft a thesis that explains the point of the narrative and the larger meaning. Use active voice. Don't just summarize in the conclusion. Explain why the story matters.
Argument essay	History	Compare political power in ancient and medieval times. Describe power, and compare it on several points. Argue which is better.	Specific explanations and examples from the textbook and lectures	Develop a thesis that states the purpose and takes a position. Provide a brief description of the historical context. Compare and contrast three or four main points about each system with evidence.	Don't use first person or offer personal opinion. Avoid passive voice. Do not use contractions. Use past tense. Use *Chicago* style.
Argument essay	English	Take a position for or against a topical issue. Describe reasons for and against your position. Explain why your reasons are better.	Personal knowledge backed up with other sources as needed	Start with the context for your argument. State the thesis at the end of the introduction in one sentence, which may also include the points you'll make. In the conclusion, restate the argument and explain why the issue matters.	You may use first person. Give the strongest points first. Give opposing views either point by point or in one paragraph. Quote or paraphrase opinions from other sources if used.

Research paper	Psychology	Research and report on studies exploring the causes of autism. Describe studies that have been done and synthesize research findings around your main points.	Experiments; systematic observations; case studies	Develop a thesis that states the purpose of the paper. In your introduction, give definitions and other necessary background. Include descriptions of methods, findings, and conclusions.	Do not use first person or include personal opinions. Summarize the studies. Paraphrase sources. Do not quote. Use APA style. Do not use contractions.
Lab report	Biology	Report on an experiment. Organize the paper with subheads for review of other experiments ("literature review"), hypothesis, methods, results, and conclusions.	Systematic, objective descriptions of methods and results; other researchers' experiments, results, and conclusions	Place the hypothesis after the review of literature. Summarize the studies. Paraphrase specific points. Use quotes only rarely. Use passive voice and past tense to explain methods and results.	Use CBE documentation style. Do not use *I*. Leave out personal opinions. Do not use contractions. (Note: Some teachers require APA style. Some teachers allow the use of first person to describe methods.)
Literary analysis essay	English	Analyze a character in a novel. Explain how the character is developed and why—for example, how the character fits into the plot and theme of the novel.	Character description with details from novel (not opinion); textual examples of the character's actions, thoughts, relationship to other characters, and so on	Briefly summarize the plot. Develop a thesis that makes an argument about the character's role in the context of the theme and plot. Support your points with specific examples and details from the novel. Quotes from the text are expected.	Analyze. Don't just summarize story passages. Support your interpretations with textual evidence. Avoid personal opinions about your likes and dislikes. Don't use *I* or passive voice. Use present tense. Use MLA style.

List similarities among assignments					
List differences among assignments					

Part III

Sample Syllabi and Assignments

As you build your own syllabi and assignments, you might consult these samples in Part III. Find more models and fresh ideas at hackerhandbooks.com/teaching.

Notes

ENGLISH COMPOSITION 1010

COURSE SYLLABUS

TERM:	Spring 2010
PREREQUISITE:	Completion of DSPW 0800 or acceptable placement scores
INSTRUCTOR:	Bobbie Kilbane
PHONE:	xxx-xxx-xxxx
OFFICE HOURS:	Mon., Wed., Fri.: 10:10 a.m.–11:00 a.m. and 12:00 p.m.–3:00 p.m.
	Tues.: Language Center 9:00 a.m.–10:30 a.m.; Office 10:30 a.m.–11:00 a.m.
	Thurs.: 9:00 a.m.–10:00 a.m.
E-MAIL:	x@volstate.edu
TEXTBOOKS:	*The Bedford Handbook,* 8th edition, Diana Hacker and Nancy Sommers. Bedford/ St. Martin's, 2010.
	The Longman Writer, 7th edition, Nadall, Langan, and Comodromos, eds. Pearson, 2009.

Overarching Goals

In English Composition 1010, students will develop and organize ideas, learn an effective writing process, and acquire mastery of composition fundamentals that will apply to a variety of writing situations throughout their academic and professional careers. English Composition 1010 will provide opportunities for students to discuss writing with instructors and peers in a safe and respectful learning environment.

Learning Objectives

Upon completing English Composition 1010, the student will be able to
- Organize essays that explain or describe a topic, narrate a personal experience, reflect on observations, and write an analysis
- Follow a process for writing an effective essay, apply invention strategies, revise drafts, and incorporate peer feedback
- Read and respond to different types of essays, observing rhetorical structure (reading as a writer)
- Identify and correct mechanical errors as part of the revision/editing process
- Analyze and comment on in-process writing, recognizing elements of strength and areas for improvement in written drafts
- Incorporate self-assessment and reflection into the writing process
- Integrate quotations, paraphrases, and summaries into his or her own writing and document them appropriately

Course Requirements

- Complete reading assignments before class (expect daily quizzes).
- Following a systematic writing process, compose four essays, two to four pages long, typed and double-spaced. Types of essays include personal narrative or description, comparison-contrast, cause-and-effect analysis, classification-division, and a research essay.
- Have a rough draft on the due date for a peer review (draft exchange).
- Maintain a course folder that includes all drafts of each essay.
- Attend at least one scheduled conference with instructor; you must bring an in-process draft of an essay.
- Avoid plagiarism—that is, using someone else's writing without acknowledging the source (see handout on plagiarism).

Bobbie Kilbane, Volunteer State Community College

Attendance and Participation

On the negative side:
- More than three absences require written evidence (such as a doctor's excuse) that the student is unable to attend class. Each unexcused absence over four is figured into the student's average as a zero.
- Coming in late three times will lower your grade.
- Missing a scheduled conference will drop your grade one letter.
- Turning in late assignments must be arranged in advance with the instructor.
- Using any electronic devices or cell phones in class or leaving class to answer a call is not allowed.
- Coming to class without an assigned rough draft when we are working with the draft in class will be counted as a zero for the day.
- Behavior that suggests that the class is not important (sleeping, eating, chewing tobacco, leaving early) is not acceptable, and you will be asked to leave.

On the positive side:
- Be on time.
- Bring materials to class (use a dictionary for reading and writing assignments).
- Prepare for each class (READ ASSIGNMENTS).
- Participate in class and small group discussions.
- Ask your instructor for help or clarification; schedule a conference if necessary.
- Communicate with your instructor by e-mail.

Instructional Methods

- Small group discussions of written in-process drafts
- Class activities with full-class participation expected
- Mini-workshops on mechanics (troubleshooting)
- Conferences
- Brief lectures
- In-class writing

Evaluation

The final course grade will be based on the following:
- A course folder containing class notes, reflections on the readings and related topics, in-process drafts, daily quizzes, and other assignments=20%
- Four essays at 15% each + writing sample essay=60%
- Final portfolio (containing a final revision of each essay) and final essay=20%

The course folder and daily quizzes (20% of final grade) will include
- All rough drafts of each essay numbered to correspond to the final draft
- The graded final draft of each essay
- Rules Lists for each graded assignment
- Quizzes and reflections on readings

The final portfolio (20% of final grade):
- The final portfolio should contain final, revised drafts of all four essays and your final examination essay, which is written in class.
- The final portfolio will be graded on improvement of writing from the beginning to the end of English Composition 1010.
- The final portfolio is a pocket folder with the four final drafts on one side and the final examination paper on the other side.
- The final portfolio is worth 20% of the final grade.

Bobbie Kilbane, Volunteer State Community College

Conferences

Conferences are meant to help students work on their own drafts. The instructor will not edit the draft and will only suggest revisions or improvements to the student. In the conference the instructor will serve as an informed member of the student's audience. Students will answer the following questions:

- What pleases you the most about this draft?
- What areas need more work?
- What changes are you considering?
- What questions would you like to ask me about the draft?

At the end of the course, students are required to meet with the instructor to review the course folder and discuss the scope, improvement, and quality of their writing for the whole semester.

ADA and Equal Opportunity Statement

In compliance with the Americans with Disabilities Act, it is the student's responsibility to disclose any disability to the Office of Disability Services to receive assistance with accommodations. It is the intent of VSCC to be free of discrimination or harassment on the basis of sex, race, color, religion, age, disability, political affiliation, sexual orientation, veteran status, or physical appearance.

Plagiarism Statement

According to the *Volunteer State Community College Student Handbook,* "Plagiarism is using other people's ideas as your own, copying all or parts of someone else's work, having another person write the assignment, getting too much assistance in writing, or failing to document accurately the use of source material" (14). Plagiarism is punishable by possible failure in the course, to be judged by the teacher, and a definite zero on the project. Students are responsible for seeking help if they are unsure about how or when to cite sources; ignorance of the rules is not a justification for plagiarism.

Financial Aid Statement

Students who are receiving Title IV financial assistance (Pell Grant, Student Loan, or SEOG Grant) must regularly attend class (a minimum of the first full week) or be subject to repay PART or ALL of the Federal Financial Aid received for the semester.

Bobbie Kilbane, Volunteer State Community College

Assignment Schedule

English Composition 1010, Section 23

From Feb. 9, 2010 through May 4, 2010

Tues. Feb. 9:

- Essay 1 due
- Sentence Patterns Workshop (based on *The Bedford Handbook*)
- Assignment Guidelines Narrative Essay (2)

Thurs. Feb. 11:

- "4th of July" LW pp. 208-211
- "Charity Display" LW pp. 220-222

Tues. Feb. 16:

- "Shooting an Elephant" LW 213-218
- Mechanics Workshop (based on *The Bedford Handbook*)
- Return Essay 1

Thurs. Feb. 18:

- Chapter 8 LW "Revising Sentences and Words" pp. 110-135
- Activities 1 through 5 pp. 135-137

Tues. Feb. 23:

- Rules List on Essay 1 due (based on *The Bedford Handbook*)
- Student Models
- Mechanics Workshop (based on *The Bedford Handbook*)

Thurs. Feb. 25:

- No Class – Department Meeting

Tues. Mar. 2:

- Rough Draft Exchange – Narrative Essay (bring *The Bedford Handbook*)

Thurs. Mar. 4:

- Essay 2 (Narrative) due
- Chapter 15 "Writing Comparison-Contrast" LW pp. 346-362
- Assignment Guidelines—Comparison-Contrast

Spring Break March 8 through March 12

Tues. Mar. 16:

- "Slow Walk of Trees" LW pp. 362-364
- Return Graded Essay 2

Bobbie Kilbane, Volunteer State Community College

Thurs. Mar. 18:

- "Reality TV" LW pp. 370-372
- "Euromail and Amerimail" LW pp. 374-377

Tues. Mar. 23:

- Class Cancelled – Conference

Thurs. Mar. 25:

- Rough Draft Exchange Essay 3 Comparison-Contrast (bring *The Bedford Handbook*)
- Rules List on Essay 2 due (based on *The Bedford Handbook*)
- Assignment Guidelines – Research Project

Tues. Mar. 30:

- Meet in Library to Begin Research
- **Final Draft of Essay 3 due**

Thurs. Apr. 1:

- Meet in Library – Database Exercise/Group Members Assigned
- Chapter 16 "Cause and Effect" LW pp. 382-400 (quiz)

Tues. Apr. 6:

- Meet in Library – Problem Selection/Group Work on Research
- Return Graded Essay 3

Thurs. Apr. 8:

- Meet in Library – Groups Work on Research
- Documenting a Research Paper/*The Bedford Handbook* Section 53 MLA

Tues. Apr. 13:

- "Why We Crave Horror Movies" LW pp. 402-405
- Documenting a Research Paper/*The Bedford Handbook* Section 53 MLA
- Rules List on Essay 3 due

Thurs. Apr. 15:

- "Innocents Afield" LW pp. 407-409 and "Black Men and Public Space" LW pp. 412-414
- Exchange Rough Drafts of Individual Research Essays (bring *The Bedford Handbook*)

Tues. Apr. 20:

- **Individual Research Essays due**
- **Start Group Presentations**

Thurs. Apr. 22:

- Group Presentations

Tues. Apr. 27 and Thurs. Apr. 29:

- Conferences (individuals to be scheduled)
- Return Graded Essay 4

Bobbie Kilbane, Volunteer State Community College

Tues. May 4:

- **Final Exam – 10:30 – 12:30**
- **Final Portfolios due (include four revised essays)**

Bobbie Kilbane, Volunteer State Community College

ENGL 1A: College Composition and Reading (4 Units, Section 6441)
Course Syllabus, Fall 2011

Instructor:	Kevin Ferns
E-mail:	x@yccd.edu
Voicemail:	xxx-xxx-xxxx
Class Time and Location:	Monday and Wednesday, 9:00–10:50 a.m., Room 801
	(Writing Lab: Wednesday, 10:00–10:50 a.m., Room 845)
Office Hours and Location:	M/W, 11:00 a.m.–12:50 p.m. and 3:00–4:00 p.m.; T/Th,
	9:00–10:20 a.m. and 3:00–4:00 p.m.; or by appointment, Room 853C

REQUIRED MATERIALS

- Hacker, Diana, and Nancy Sommers. *Rules for Writers*, 7th ed. Boston: Bedford/St. Martin's, 2012. ISBN 0-312-64736-0.
- Muller, Gilbert. *The McGraw-Hill Reader*, 10th ed. Boston: McGraw-Hill, 2008. ISBN 978-0-07-353313-1.
- A good dictionary. You might try *Merriam Webster's Collegiate Dictionary*, 11th ed., although this one can be hefty. A lighter and cheaper model is the pocket *American Heritage Dictionary* (less than $10 in our bookstore).
- A notebook or binder for recording notes, ideas, and freewrites (and to hold this syllabus).

Be sure to purchase the updated editions listed and bring all course materials to each class. If you need to make copies of assigned pages until you obtain your own copies of each text, these texts are on reserve in the library (for library use only).

COURSE PREREQUISITE

Satisfactory score on the Placement Examination and appropriate skills and knowledge or a grade of C or better in English 51.

COURSE OVERVIEW

> "I write to find out what I'm thinking. I write to find out who I am.
> I write to understand things."
> —Julia Alvarez

> "Writing and rewriting are a constant search for what one is saying." —John Updike

English 1A is dedicated to reading, writing, and discussion to improve critical thinking and writing skills. You will explore the craft and process of writing and produce several original essays that demonstrate excellence in critical analysis, organization, and development. This course will emphasize critical thinking skills, and our primary focus will fall on skills required across disciplines (namely, the ability to understand and respond to a text, to develop and defend your own ideas, and to integrate sources with your own thinking). We will also consider mechanical and grammatical issues, and you will be responsible for observing the rules of standard English in all of the coursework you do. When you have completed this course, you will have written more than 5,000 words of formal writing and more than 20,000 words online, and you will be comfortable using formal research techniques to synthesize ideas from various sources to inform your opinion on a topic.

GRADES

Your final grade will be assessed based on your performance in four areas:

→

1. Quizzes, 10%   Quizzes may be administered at the beginning of class on assigned readings.

2. Responses, 20%   This includes in-class assignments and discussions on WebCT.

3. Exams, 30%   Two midterm essay exams and a final in-class essay exam are required.

4. Essays, 40%   Four draft and final essays are required.

A final grade of 90 percent or higher earns an A; 80 to 89 percent earns a B; 70 to 79 percent earns a C; and 60 to 69 percent earns a D. All grades are non-negotiable. If you are concerned about your progress in this class or would like to know your status, please e-mail me or see me during office hours, and we can discuss what you can do to improve your writing. We will be meeting during the writing labs to discuss your writing as well.

Quizzes (10%): Thoughtful critical reading is essential to your development as a writer, and you must make an effort to understand assigned readings before coming to class. At the beginning of class, a quiz may be given to assess your understanding of or engagement with assigned readings or lessons. I will use quizzes as a means to assess your progress and understanding of course material throughout the semester. If you miss a class or are late on the day a quiz is given, you will receive a zero for that quiz. You cannot make it up at a later date. Quizzes will be periodically returned to you with minimal comments and will be assessed on a check plus (outstanding response)/check (average response)/check minus (more effort needed) basis. This assessment will be converted to a percentage of your grade at the end of the semester. If you do not miss any quizzes and consistently earn check plus or check marks, you will receive an A or a B for this segment of your grade.

Responses and replies on WebCT and in-class writing assignments (20%): Prior to most class days, I will provide on WebCT a question or questions in the Discussions area related to the assigned readings. (To access WebCT, go to www.yccd.edu, click on Online/ITV, and then click on the WebCT Log-in button.) Your responses represent your initial informal thoughts, and this informal writing will help prepare you for the class discussion on the readings. In the response, you are writing to learn, so you can take chances, push yourself in new directions, and be creative with this writing. Your response will be viewed by your classmates; therefore, I expect you to maintain the attention to grammar, spelling, and critical thought (not to mention respect for fellow classmates) that you would show in essays and in class discussion. Before each class period, you will be required to log on to WebCT and post one response to this prompt (250-word minimum; type in the word count at the end of the post) and two paragraph-long replies to your classmates. Your responses and replies will be assessed on a credit or no-credit basis and converted to a percentage of your grade at the end of the semester. All response questions will be posted at least two days in advance of the due date, so you will have ample time to post your responses and replies. I will read your responses and reply privately at my discretion. Responses will not be accepted more than one week after the due date, so it is imperative that you keep up with the readings and responses. If you submit complete responses and replies on time, you will receive an A for this segment of your grade. Late or short responses are worth half credit, and failure to submit a response or replies to other students earns you a zero for that response. If you consistently fail to submit responses on time, you will not pass the class.

Exams (30%): You will write two in-class essays (10% each) in preparation for the English department final exam (10%). On both midterms and on the final, you will be asked to respond to a prompt in essay format. Each exam will be rated according to the rubric in this syllabus based on content, structure, organization, development of ideas, and mechanics: a 4+ is 100%, a 4 is 95%, a 4– is 90%, a 3+ is 85%, a 3 is 80%, a 3– is 75%, a 2+ is 70%, a 2 is 65%, and a 2– is 60%. Failure to complete a midterm or the final exam will result in a final grade of F for the course. I will be grading the midterm essays, but the final in-class essay will be graded by a team of professors from the WCC English department. You must maintain at least a C average (2+ or above) on this portion of your grade to pass the course.

Essays (40%): You must type and submit four draft and final essays by the beginning of class on

Kevin Ferns, Yuba Community College

the due dates listed. I will not grade your draft essays, but I will be offering advice and comments for revision, as will your peers. The essay-writing and revision process is essential to producing a successful final draft; therefore, your essay grade will be reduced if you fail to do the following:

1. Submit drafts on time.

2. Meet the minimum word count.

3. Format according to MLA guidelines.

4. Participate actively in the peer review sessions.

5. Offer written feedback for each group member during the peer reviews (and submit a copy to me via e-mail).

6. Significantly revise your essays and submit a revision summary with each final essay detailing the changes made. Each revised essay should include a one-page revision summary cover sheet. Your revision summary is an analysis of how you revised your essay based on the information you received from your peers and/or instructor. In the revision summary, you should reflect on your writing process by identifying at least one writing problem you needed to solve as you revised (other than grammar and spelling) and explaining in detail how you solved it. In addition, you should discuss your revisions in the context of your essay's supporting points and organization. With your essay's purpose and audience in mind, discuss how you improved your writing. Your revision summary is your final essay's cover letter to me explaining how and why your essay is stronger based on the revisions made.

You will receive a grade (based on the rubric in this syllabus) on each revised essay, which will be due approximately one week after each peer review workshop. Revised essays should be submitted both in hard copy on the due date and electronically via www.turnitin.com (Class ID is xxxxxxx; enrollment password is xxxxx) before class on the assigned due date. Essays are always due at the beginning of class. Essays submitted late will be penalized up to half of the total essay grade. If you fail to turn in an essay or submit an essay more than one week late, you will receive an F grade for the course.

Some advice on grades: Keep in mind that your final letter grade will not have a plus or minus after it. Therefore, when it comes to borderline grades, the difference between rounding up to an A or down to a B may depend on whether you made a noticeable effort to improve in this class. I do notice such things as perfect attendance, thoughtful and enthusiastic participation in class discussions, careful attention to revisions in your writing, and a willingness to work hard consistently, and these qualities could make the difference between a passing grade and a failing one.

COURSE EXPECTATIONS

Attendance: The class experience is an essential component of your education, and your participation is vital to successful class discussions and activities. Therefore, attendance is required. I understand that emergencies sometimes occur, and you will be allowed three absences over the course of the semester. (I make no distinction between excused and unexcused absences, so please use your absences wisely.) Please arrive before the beginning of class and remain in class until you are dismissed. If you arrive excessively late or depart before the end of class, you will be considered absent for the day. If you are late or absent, you will be expected to follow up with a trusted classmate to determine what you have missed. If you miss more than three classes, your grade will drop one letter grade for each additional missed class (thus, an A student would earn a D on a sixth absence).

Academic integrity: As a student at Woodland Community College, you join a community of scholars committed to excellence in the teaching and learning process. I assume that you will pursue your studies with integrity and honesty, meaning you will never appropriate another person's words, thoughts, ideas, or data as your own. Plagiarism includes the following:

Kevin Ferns, Yuba Community College

- Failure to properly cite the source of any material borrowed from an outside source (such as books, periodicals, and the Internet), including failure to use quotation marks to distinguish another author's exact words from your own, failure to give credit for the paraphrased ideas of others, and failure to include bibliographic information for all secondary sources used.
- Submitting any assignment not written by you for this class (such as an essay written by a friend or purchased from an online source, an essay written by you for another class, or an essay copied from a book, magazine, or other media source).

If you violate this policy, I am obligated under the Woodland Community College Student Honor Code to take disciplinary action that may include assigning an F grade for the assignment or an F grade for the course. Depending on the severity of the infraction, you may also be placed on disciplinary probation. If you have any questions or concerns regarding how to incorporate sources correctly or avoid plagiarism, please see me for assistance.

ADDITIONAL WRITING ASSISTANCE

Your success in this class depends on your commitment to improvement. I recommend that you take advantage of the opportunities available on the WCC campus at the Tutoring Center (Room 809). You can sign up for free peer tutoring to help you identify and prioritize your goals to improve your writing. You can also visit the English Writing Lab (Room 850) to work individually on your essays with the instructional assistant to improve your writing. I recommend that you sign up for these services early in the semester for maximum benefit. The longer you wait, the more difficult it is to make significant progress with your writing.

ACCOMMODATIONS

If you have a learning disability, please provide the appropriate documentation as soon as possible to ensure that you receive the necessary accommodations. This information will be kept confidential.

ELECTRONIC DEVICES

Please turn off and put away your phone, iPod, laptop computer, and any other electronic devices before entering the classroom.

FOOD

Please do not bring food into the classroom. Bottled beverages and coffee with a secure cap are permissible. Food and drink are not allowed in the computer labs.

GUESTS

Please do not bring your friends, pets, or children to class.

COMMITMENT

Whether you are reading, writing, or discussing your thoughts, your development as a writer depends on your commitment to each class activity. This course will demand a great deal of your time and effort over the next 16 weeks, and you will need to prioritize this class to make measurable progress. If you come to class every day prepared to participate and contribute, turn in assignments on time, and take an obvious interest in your work and in improving your writing ability, you will most likely succeed in this course.

OUT-OF-CLASS ESSAY SCORING RUBRIC

C   =   **Content, 25%**
O   =   **Organization, 25%**
M   =   **Mechanics and Punctuation, 25%**
P   =   **Process, 25%**

Kevin Ferns, Yuba Community College

A = **A superior essay** (90–100 total; 23–25 per category) is fresh, personal, and engaging and includes the following:

C: A well-chosen thesis clearly controls the direction of the paper; supporting points are thoroughly developed with clear, well-chosen, vivid examples; analysis of the subject is clear, thorough, and logical; the intended audience's needs are fulfilled.

O: Paragraphs exhibit unity and coherence; organization is smooth and logical.

M: Diction and tone are appropriate and exhibit flair and demonstrate superior control; sentence structure is varied and superbly managed; few, if any, errors in mechanics exist.

P: Essay has correct formatting; all drafts, revisions, revision summary, and peer review materials are submitted on time with word count met; workshops are attended; significant revisions are made successfully.

B = **A strong essay** (80–89 total; 20–22 per category) is above average and succeeds at most of the following:

C: Thesis is clear and worthwhile, and it controls the essay's direction; analysis is clear and logical, with only rare lapses; examples are well chosen but may occasionally be lacking in specificity or vividness.

O: Organization is generally clear and logical; paragraphs support the thesis and are generally unified and coherent.

M: Essay may contain a few errors or some ineffective sentences, but other sentences will show flair; essay generally shows evidence of careful proofreading (overall freedom from mechanical errors).

P: Essay has decent formatting; all drafts, revisions, revision summary, and peer review materials are submitted on time; workshops are attended; most revisions are made successfully.

C = **An adequate essay** (70–79 total; 18–19 per category) is average and includes the following:

C: The topic is very worthy of development in a college essay; essay generally features an appropriate tone for the assignment and intended audience; examples might be sparse and/or occasionally not quite to the point; the essay is primarily analytical, but the writer might depend at some points on narration where analysis is required.

O: Organization is generally clear but sometimes formulaic; paragraphs support the thesis, but some might lack unity or coherence.

M: Sentence structure might be choppy or lack variety; essay is generally free of errors in spelling, punctuation, and capitalization; occasional errors don't impede understanding.

P: Essay has some formatting errors; most drafts, revisions, and peer review materials/workshops are submitted on time; word count may not be met; revision summary is too brief/lacks specificity, or not all revisions are made successfully.

D = **A marginal essay** (60–69 total; 15–17 per category) is below average and does the following:

C: Essay responds simplistically to prompt; thesis is not clearly stated.

O: Paragraphs may lack focus and wander from the point or not advance the thesis, mostly summarize, lack a controlling idea, have little or no analysis, or have little development.

M: Sentences lack variety; significant proofreading, mechanical, and spelling errors are present.

P: Essay has formatting errors; drafts, revisions, revision summary, and/or peer review materials are submitted late; workshops are not attended, or revisions are not made successfully; word counts are not met.

Kevin Ferns, Yuba Community College

F = A failing essay (0–59 total; less than 15 per category)

The F essay is a clear fail that misunderstands the point of the assignment; lacks direction; is unduly brief; lacks development and coherence; or contains numerous spelling, punctuation, or grammar errors. Late submission or a lack of emphasis on the revision process and peer reviews can lead to an F paper as well.

IN-CLASS ESSAY SCORING RUBRIC

4 to 4+ (95–100%): A superior essay demonstrates a clear ability to go beyond the basics of the assignment and shows mastery of the critical thinking abilities that are required to understand, interpret, and argue the topic. In addition, it has only minor flaws. An essay in this category does the following:

- It addresses the topic clearly and responds effectively to all aspects of the task.
- It states or clearly implies the writer's position or thesis and provides in-depth analysis of the source essay.
- The response is clearly and logically organized with ideas supported by relevant reasons, well-chosen examples, strong transitions, and concrete details.
- The essay explores the issues thoughtfully and in depth without redundancy.
- Quoted passages or references to a source text are explained and credited to the author.
- Word choice is appropriate to the essay's audience and purpose and may show some flair.

3+ to 4– (85–90%): A strong essay demonstrates clear competence in writing by going beyond just the basic requirements of the assignment and demonstrating an ability to critically understand, interpret, and argue the topic. It may have some errors, but they are not serious enough to distract or confuse the reader. An essay in this category does the following:

- Clearly addresses the topic but may respond to some aspects of the task more effectively than others
- States or clearly implies the writer's position or thesis with strong analysis of the source essay's appeals
- Is clearly and logically organized and developed with relevant reasons and examples
- Shows some depth and complexity by explaining thoroughly while avoiding redundancy
- Displays syntactic variety and maintains appropriate vocabulary
- Credits to the author any quoted passages or references
- May have a few errors in grammar, mechanics, or usage

3– to 3 (75–80%): An adequate essay completes the basic requirements of the assignment. It may have some errors that distract the reader, but these errors do not significantly impede understanding. An essay in this category does the following:

- Addresses the topic but may slight some aspects of the task
- States or implies the writer's position or thesis with average analysis of the source text
- Is adequately organized and developed, generally supporting ideas with reasons, examples, and details
- Treats the topic simplistically or superficially and without depth, or may repeat ideas
- Displays some syntactic variety and maintains appropriate vocabulary
- May have some errors in grammar, mechanics, and/or usage

2 to 2+ (65–70%): A marginal essay demonstrates developing competence but may lack analytical insight into the topic or appropriate development, given the purpose of the essay. An essay in this category does the following:

- Distorts, neglects, or ignores aspects of the task and may confuse some aspects of the source essay
- Announces the topic but lacks a stated or implied position or thesis
- Lacks focus and demonstrates confused or illogical thinking
- Is poorly organized or developed, has weak or irrelevant details, and may contain factual errors
- Has problems with syntactic variety, simplistic or inappropriate vocabulary, and an accumulation of errors in grammar, mechanics, and usage such that it impedes understanding

Kevin Ferns, Yuba Community College

1 to 2– (50–60%): A weak essay suggests possible difficulties in reading and writing and may have one or more of the following weaknesses:

- The essay displays confusion about the topic or ignores important aspects of the task; it lacks a thesis.
- It provides simplistic generalizations without support and has weak organization.
- Errors in grammar, mechanics, and usage impede reader understanding.

ENGLISH 1A COURSE SCHEDULE

The course schedule is designed to be flexible to meet your needs. The following assignments will be modified and detailed as we progress, and I will notify you as we make updates and changes to this schedule throughout the semester. I will list specific homework and reading response assignments on the board at the beginning of each class session and on WebCT. Page numbers refer to *The McGraw-Hill Reader* unless *Rules for Writers* is specified.

Date	Class Topic	Essays and Workshops
Mon., 8/15	Course Introduction	Writing history essay
Wed., 8/17	"Critical Thinking, Reading, and Writing" (2–11); Adler, "How to Mark a Book" (57–61); Elbow, "Freewriting" (68–71)	Writing Lab; Introduction to WebCT
Mon., 8/22	"Critical Thinking, Reading, and Writing" (11–27)	Essay 1 assigned: Evaluation and Response
Wed., 8/24	*Rules for Writers*, Chapter 5 (70–83); "Critical Thinking, Reading, and Writing" (32–54)	Writing Lab
Mon., 8/29	"Reading and Writing Effective Arguments" (104–114 and 126–129); *Rules for Writers*, Chapter 7 (102–110)	Writing Lab
Wed., 8/31	"The Penalty of Death" and "The Death Penalty Is a Step Back" (145–150)	
Mon., 9/5	Labor Day (No Class)	
Wed., 9/7	"Debate: Animal Research" (154–158)	Writing Lab
Mon., 9/12	"Debate: The Patriot Act" (160–170)	
Wed., 9/14	"Debate: The Patriot Act" (171–175)	Writing Lab; Essay 1 draft due (4 copies)
Mon., 9/19	"Critical Thinking, Reading, and Writing" (54–56)	Peer review workshop; peer essay evaluations due
Wed., 9/21	"Reading and Writing Effective Arguments" (117–126 and 129–143); *Rules for Writers*, Chapter 6 (84–101)	Writing Lab; Essay 2 assigned: Health and Medicine
Mon., 9/26	Midterm Exam 1: Evaluation and Response	Essay 1 final due with revision summary; submit to www.turnitin.com
Wed., 9/28	"Writing a Research Paper" (178–232); *Rules for Writers*, Chapters 53–60 (420–532)	Writing Lab

Kevin Ferns, Yuba Community College

Date	Class Topic	Essays and Workshops
Mon., 10/3	"This Is the End of the World" (733–741)	
Wed., 10/5	"We Are Not Immune" (742–751)	Writing Lab
Mon., 10/10	"The Terrifying Normalcy of AIDS" (760–763); "The Globalization of Eating Disorders" (787–790)	
Wed., 10/12	"The Man Who Couldn't Stop Eating" (764–777)	Writing Lab; Essay 2 draft due (4 copies)
Mon., 10/17		Peer review workshop; peer essay evaluations due
Wed., 10/19	"Why Are We Fascinated by Gangsters?" (558–575)	Essay 3 assigned: Media and Popular Culture
Mon., 10/24	Midterm Exam 2: Evaluation and Response	Essay 2 final due with revision summary; submit to www.turnitin.com
Wed., 10/26	"My Creature from the Black Lagoon" (582–589)	Writing Lab
Mon., 10/31	"Wonder Woman" (593–601)	
Wed., 11/2	"Escape from Wonderland" (610–622)	Writing Lab
Mon., 11/7	"Loose Ends" (577–578); "Supersaturation" (602–608)	
Wed., 11/9	"Red, White, and Beer" (590–592); "Analyzing Visual Texts" (28–32) and "An Album of Advertisements: Images of Culture"	Writing Lab; Essay 3 draft due (4 copies)
Mon., 11/14		Peer review workshop; peer essay evaluations due
Wed., 11/16	"Superstition" (676–686)	Essay 4 assigned: Philosophy, Ethics, and Religion
Mon., 11/21	"I Listen to My Parents and I Wonder What They Believe" (688–692); "Salvation" (693–695)	Essay 3 final due with revision summary; submit to www.turnitin.com
Wed., 11/23	Thanksgiving (No Class)	
Mon., 11/28	"The Allegory of the Cave" (704–707)	
Wed., 11/30	"The Culture of Disbelief" (716–724); "Not about Islam?" (709–711)	Essay 4 draft due (4 copies)
Mon., 12/5		Peer review workshop; peer essay evaluations due
Wed., 12/7	Final Exam Review	
Thurs., 12/8	Final Exam, Evaluation and Response, 8:00–11:00 a.m., Room TBA	Essay 4 final due with revision summary; submit to www.turnitin.com

Kevin Ferns, Yuba Community College

English 101: Syllabus

Instructor:	Sheena Denney Boran
E-mail:	x@olemiss.edu
Office:	Somerville x
Office hours:	MW 3-4, and by appointment

Course Texts

Bullock, Richard, and Maureen Daly Goggin, eds. *The Norton Field Guide to Writing, with Readings.* 2nd ed. New York: W. W. Norton & Company, 2009.

Hacker, Diana, and Nancy Sommers. *A Writer's Reference.* 7th ed. Boston: Bedford/St. Martin's, 2011.

Note: Readings outside the texts will be posted on Blackboard under Readings. *You will be required to print out copies of the materials and bring them to class on the assigned dates. More information will be given in class.*

Course Description

This course will assist students in recognizing and understanding different audiences and rhetorical purposes for reaching those audiences. Throughout the course, students will be assigned readings and participate in class discussions that serve to illuminate potential rhetorical purposes. In addition, students will regularly use a writing process that nurtures ideas and develops texts over time; the semester will feature major assignments from five different genres culminating in a portfolio project that serves to highlight this writing process. The assigned work in English 101 should prove simultaneously challenging and interesting and encourage students to work with their peers and their instructor in better understanding how the written language functions academically, professionally, and privately. To that end, students will examine ideas (both their own and those of others) critically, engage in reflective practices, begin to interact with and document secondary source material in anticipation of English 102, and learn to better understand and navigate the standard conventions of academic English.

Student Learning Outcomes

1. Students will demonstrate writing as a process that requires brainstorming, drafting, revising, editing, and proofreading.

2. Students will use writing to respond to readings, to explore unfamiliar ideas, to question thinking different from their own, to reflect on personal experiences, and to develop sound arguments.

3. Students will produce writing suitable for a variety of purposes, with an emphasis on academic purposes.

4. Students will integrate primary sources with their own ideas through summary, paraphrase, and quotation, and document those sources properly.

5. Students will produce writing that is free of serious grammatical and mechanical errors.

Grading

Memoir	10%
In-Class Essay	5%
Advertisement Analysis	15%

Sheena Denney Boran, University of Mississippi

Position Argument	20%
Photo/ Image Essay	15%
Homework/Class Participation	10%
Portfolio	25%

Major Due Dates

Monday, February 14 – Memoir Due

Wednesday, February 23 – In-class Essay

Monday, March 21 – Advertisement Analysis Due

Monday, April 4 – Position Argument Due

Monday, April 18 – Photo/Image Essay Due

Monday, May 2 – Portfolio Due

Attendance Policy

Students are expected to attend all class meetings; improving writing skills takes time and is a process unlike learning content alone. In acknowledgment of the fact that students may experience some circumstances which prevent complete attendance, the following policy is in effect:

MWF Courses

1 day missed: no penalty

2 days missed: no penalty

3 days missed: no penalty

4 days missed: no penalty

5 days missed: final course grade lowered by one letter grade

6 days missed: final course grade lowered by two letter grades

7 days missed: final course grade lowered by three letter grades

8 days missed: failure

There will be no excused or unexcused absences.

Late Work Policy

Due to the structured nature of this class, late work is unacceptable. If you are aware that you will be unable to meet a deadline, contact the instructor prior to the assignment due date.

Classroom Decorum

The classroom is a place of learning; others are paying to be here too. Please make sure not to distract others from learning and to respect the opinions of others. From time to time we will review each other's writing in peer review sessions. Please follow the guideline of being a "critical friend" in all of your responses to classmates' work. Students who cannot adhere to these behavioral expectations are subject to discipline in accordance with the procedures described in the M Book.

Disabilities

If you have a documented disability as described by the Rehabilitation Act of 1973 (P.L. 933-112 Section 504) or the Americans with Disabilities Act (ADA) and would like to request academic and/ or physical accommodations please contact Student Disability Services at 234 Martindale Center, xxx-xxx-xxxx. Course requirements will not be waived but reasonable accommodations may be provided as appropriate.

Plagiarism

All work that you submit under your name for credit at UM is assumed to be your original work. While teachers hope and expect that you will incorporate the thinking of others in your work, you must credit others' work when you rely upon it. In your written assignments, there are only three methods for properly integrating the work of others: quotation, paraphrase, and summary (see pp. 361-365, 376-379, 448-451, and 502-504 in *A Writer's Reference*).

The penalty for plagiarism in English 101 is failure of the course. Additional penalties are possible.

Policies Subject to Change

All information in this syllabus is subject to change at any time, especially during the first weeks of the semester. I will announce changes to our schedule during class time and also via Blackboard. You are responsible for changes to the schedule as they arise, regardless of whether or not you attend class.

DAILY SCHEDULE OF ACTIVITIES

Week One	
Mon., Jan. 24	Class introductions, Bios *HW: Read Robert Atwan on Opinion and Participating in Class Discussion (Blackboard)*
Wed., Jan. 26	Opinion Exercise, How to Talk in Class *HW: Discussion prompt response: "How I Write Papers." Bring to Friday's class.*
Fri., Jan. 28	College Writing, Chalk & Wire *HW: Read pp. 153-160 in* Norton.
Week Two	
Mon., Jan. 31	Introduction to Memoir, Brainstorming *HW: Choose the central event for your memoir, and write down everything you can remember about it. Read pp. 343-349 and pp. 826-830 in* Norton *and section C1-b in* A Writer's Reference.
Wed., Feb. 2	Drafting the Memoir, Narrating *HW: Select a narrative strategy for your memoir, and produce a rough draft that conforms to that narrative strategy, making appropriate use of time markers and transitions. Read pp. 324-332 and pp. 802-808 in* Norton *and p. 35 in* A Writer's Reference.
Fri., Feb. 4	Revising the Memoir, Describing *HW: Examine your own memoir and add sensory details. Read pp. 261-270 and pp. 819-824 in* Norton *and p. 36 in* A Writer's Reference.

Sheena Denney Boran, University of Mississippi

Week Three	
Mon., Feb. 7	Revising the Memoir, Beginning and Ending *HW: Select appropriate beginning and ending strategies for your memoir. Revise accordingly. Be sure to revise transitions throughout your memoir so that it flows smoothly from beginning to end. Read sections C2 and C3 and pp. 32-33 in* A Writer's Reference.
Wed., Feb. 9	Memoir Peer Review *HW: Read pp. 367-372 in* Norton *and p. 22, Guidelines for peer reviewers, in* A Writer's Reference.
Fri., Feb. 11	**Class Canceled – Conferences**
Week Four	
Mon.,Feb. 14	**Paper One Due (Memoir)** Introduction to In-Class Essay, The Writing Process *HW: Read sample in-class essays (Blackboard)*
Wed.,Feb. 16	Reading Questions & Outlining *HW: Read pp. 272-277 in* Norton *and section C1-d in* A Writer's Reference.
Fri., Feb. 18	In-Class Essay, Guiding the Reader *HW: Read pp. 653-657 in* Norton.
Week Five	
Mon., Feb. 21	Practice In-Class Essay *HW: Reading TBA*
Wed., Feb. 23	**Paper Two Due (in class essay)** *HW: Read pp. 38 and 43-58 in* Norton.
Fri., Feb. 25	Introduction to Advertisement Analysis *HW: Read pp. 325-366 and 604-608 in* Norton *and pp. 68, 70, and 77 in* A Writer's Reference. *Begin searching for an advertisement to analyze in your essay.*
Week Six	
Mon., Feb. 28	Practice Advertisement Analysis *HW: Choose an advertisement (or group of advertisements) to analyze in your essay. Summarize the content of the advertisement in a brief paragraph. Read Rebecca Hollingsworth's "An Imperfect Reality" (Blackboard)*
Wed., Mar. 2	Drafting the Advertisement Analysis *HW: Read p. 70 and the outline on p. 72 in* A Writer's Reference. *Begin drafting analysis of your advertisement, making use of image analysis terms.*
Fri., Mar. 4	Drafting the Advertisement Analysis *HW: Read section A3-a in* A Writer's Reference. *Examine your advertisement for each of the appeals, as well as logical fallacies and underlying cultural assumptions. Revise your analysis to include this new information.*

Sheena Denney Boran, University of Mississippi

Week Seven	
Mon., Mar. 7	**Class Canceled – Conferences**
Wed., Mar. 9	**Class Canceled – Conferences**
Fri., Mar. 11	Advertisement Analysis Peer Review *Bring to class two hard copies of your Advertisement Analysis and two copies of the peer review sheet (Blackboard).* *HW: Read pp. 83-110 in* Norton.
Week Eight	
Mon., Mar. 14	**Spring break, no class**
Wed., Mar. 16	**Spring break, no class**
Fri., Mar. 18	**Spring break, no class**
Week Nine	
Mon., Mar. 21	**Paper Three Due (Advertisement Analysis)** Introduction to Position Argument *HW: Read pp. 283-299 and pp. 666-676 in* Norton. *Brainstorm at least three possible issues about which to write.*
Wed., Mar. 23	Drafting the Position Argument: Logos, Ethos, Pathos *HW: Read pp. 408-419 and pp. 684-695 in* Norton. *Choose the issue for your argument essay and generate a position statement.*
Fri., Mar. 25	Drafting the Position Argument: Quotation, Paraphrase, Summary *HW: Read pp. 67-85 in* A Writer's Reference *and Ann Marie Paulin's "Cruelty, Civility, and Other Weighty Matters" (Blackboard). Begin drafting Position Argument, focusing on what others say.*
Week Ten	
Mon., Mar. 28	Drafting the Position Argument: Responding to Others *HW: Read pp. 697-716 in* Norton *and section A2-f in* A Writer's Reference. *Continue drafting Position Argument, focusing on your own position.*
Wed., Mar. 30	Revising the Position Argument *HW: Read chapter C3 in* A Writer's Reference. *Revise Position Argument.*
Fri., Apr. 1	Position Argument Peer Review *Bring to class two hard copies of your Position Argument and two copies of the peer review sheet (Blackboard)*
Week Eleven	
Mon., Apr. 4	**Paper Four Due (Position Argument)** Introduction to Photo/Image Essay *HW: Read pp. 528-532 in* Norton. *Write a one-paragraph summary of the essay you want to adapt for this project.*
Wed., Apr. 6	Finding, Creating, and Using Photos and Images
Fri., Apr. 8	**Virtual Class Meeting** *HW: Collect or create at least 15 images for your essay. Read Simon Benlow's "An Apology to Future Generations" (Blackboard).*

Sheena Denney Boran, University of Mississippi

Week Twelve	
Mon., Apr. 11	Drafting the Photo/Image Essay *HW: Create a storyboard for your essay.*
Wed., Apr. 13	Revising the Photo/Image Essay *HW: Review chapter C3 in* A Writer's Reference.
Fri., Apr. 15	Photo/Image Essay Peer Review *Bring to class two hard copies of your Photo/Image Essay and two copies of the peer review sheet (Blackboard).*
Week Thirteen	
Mon., Apr. 18	**Photo/Image Essay Due** Photo/Image Essay Presentations
Wed., Apr. 20	Photo/Image Essay Presentations
Fri., Apr. 22	Photo/Image Essay Presentations/Portfolio preparation *HW: Read section C3-e in* A Writer's Reference.
Week Fourteen	
Mon.,Apr. 25	Portfolio preparation
Wed., Apr. 27	Portfolio preparation
Fri., Apr. 29	Portfolio preparation
Week Fifteen	
Mon., May 2	Final tweaks/revision to portfolio **Portfolio Due by 5:00 PM**
Wed., May 4	Portfolio presentations
Fri., May 6	Portfolio presentations **Last day of class**

Sheena Denney Boran, University of Mississippi

English 200: ADVANCED COMPOSITION
Three Credits

Meeting Days/Times:	(88545) Tuesdays and Thursdays, 7:30 a.m. to 8:45 a.m. – HOLM 248
	(88546) Tuesdays and Thursdays, 9:00 a.m. to 10:15 a.m. – SAKAM B308
Instructor:	Jill Dahlman; x@hawaii.edu
Office:	KUY XXX
Effective Date:	Spring 2012 (January 9, 2012, through May 11, 2012)

University of Hawaii at Manoa College of Languages, Linguistics, and Literature

MISSION STATEMENT

The College of Languages, Linguistics, and Literature (LLL) places the study of language in its many manifestations at the center of its students' education. Through small classes and close student-faculty interchange, the College prepares students for lifelong learning in English studies, Hawaiian and foreign languages, and applied and theoretical linguistics. While taking a global view of language, literature, and linguistics, LLL offers a special focus on Asia-Pacific-Hawai'i.

LLL faculty conduct research and produce scholarship according to the highest standards of inquiry and creativity in the liberal arts tradition. The range of faculty interests—from the analysis of language structure, acquisition, history, and use to the creation of teaching materials for familiar as well as less commonly taught languages; from the study of classic and contemporary texts of world literatures to the production of new literatures—reflects its commitment to innovation and excellence.

CATALOG DESCRIPTION

Further study of rhetorical, conceptual, and stylistic demands of writing; instruction develops the writing and research skills covered in Composition I. Pre: 100, 100A, 101/101L, or ELI 100. NI.

Activities Required at Scheduled Times Other Than Class Times
- Homework, including but not limited to CompClass discussion board postings, quizzes, reading of short essays, and other homework that may be noted in class
- Compilation of portfolio
- Writing assignments
- Research Unit to be completed independent of class
- Frequent checking of e-mail and CompClass discussion board

STUDENT LEARNING OUTCOMES

Upon successful completion of English 200, students should be able to complete the following as independent learners. The student learning outcomes for the course are:

00. Write well-reasoned compositions that reveal the complexity of the topic students have chosen to explore or argue.

01. Read for main points, perspective, and purpose; evaluate the quality of evidence, negotiate conflicting positions, and analyze the effectiveness of a text's approach to integrate that knowledge into their writing.

02. Choose language, style, and organization appropriate to particular purposes and audiences.

03. Synthesize previous experience and knowledge with the ideas and information students discover as they read and write.

04. Use sources such as libraries and the Internet to enhance students' understanding of the ideas they explore or argue in their writing; analyze and evaluate their research for reliability, bias, and relevance.

05. Use readers' responses as one source for revising writing.

06. Use standard disciplinary conventions to integrate and document sources.

07. Edit and proofread in the later stages of the writing process, especially when writing for public audiences; control such surface features as syntax, grammar, punctuation, and spelling.

COURSE CONTENT

- **Discussion board postings** will satisfy learning outcomes 01, 03, 04, 05, and 06.
- Essays found in *Writing and Revising* and essay readings and discussions in *From Critical Thinking to Argument* will satisfy learning outcome 02.
- *A Pocket Style Manual,* **6th Edition**, will aid in satisfying learning outcomes 03, 04, 06, and 07.
- **Writing assignments**, most of which are to be completed outside of class (see course schedule for specific details), will satisfy learning outcomes 01, 03, 04, 05, 06, and 07.
- **Homework**, including quizzes, will work toward all learning outcomes.

Concepts or Topics
- Ethos, pathos, logos (and other rhetorical skills)
- Rhetoric/rhetorical situation
- The differences among audiences; how to write to be effective for each audience
- The ability to write for specific purposes and to identify purpose in the writing of others.
- Learning to dig deeply into outside material, unpack the material, and understand its deeper meaning
- Understand the difference between summarizing, paraphrasing, and plagiarism

Skills or Competencies
1. Work independently to accomplish specific tasks, such as homework, research, and writing
2. Successfully manage time in order to complete all tasks
3. Follow directions
4. Ask questions to clear up misunderstandings, clarify directions, or seek assistance on papers (if needed)
5. Understand that writing is a process that takes time in order to produce excellent work
6. Understand the importance and necessity of mastering multiple proofreading and revision techniques
7. Demonstrate respect toward the professor and classmates at all times

Jill Dahlman, University of Hawaii at Manoa College of Languages, Linguistics, and Literature

SCORING BREAKDOWN—KEEPING TRACK OF SCORES

Assignment	Grade	Out of Possible	Total
Discussion forum postings Need a total of 30 (x 3 points)		90	
Summary-Responses Need a total of 9 (x 5 points)		45	
Attendance/class participation		50	
Open-book quizzes		70	
Identity Unit • Major paper (mandatory) • Paper option(s)		40 20	
Music Unit • Major paper (mandatory) • Paper option(s)		40 20	
Star Trek Unit • Major paper (mandatory) • Paper option(s)		40 20	
Comic Book Unit • Paper option(s)		30	
Science Fiction Unit • Major paper (mandatory) • Paper option(s)		40 20	
Research Paper (all components mandatory) • Project proposal • Annotated bibliography (5 entries x 10 points) • Drafts and peer review • Project presentation • Research paper		25 50 10 50 90	
Portfolio		250	

COURSE TASKS

1. Attend each class meeting.

2. Complete all assigned readings on time.

3. Complete all assignments on time.

4. Use library resources for scholarly credibility.

5. Take the initiative to ask the instructor relevant questions both inside and outside of class.

6. Contribute to class discussions.

Jill Dahlman, University of Hawaii at Manoa College of Languages, Linguistics, and Literature

ASSIGNMENTS

Discussion Board Postings: 90 points (10%)

To become great writers, we need practice. To that end, we will be using discussion board postings in this class. Thirty (30) discussion board postings will be required (two will be due each week). There should be no concern for grammar, punctuation, paragraphs, and so on, as the purpose of these entries is to provide you with practice writing and debating with your fellow classmates. The most important part of an entry is the content. If you choose to respond to another student's posting, you must be respectful in your response. There is no tolerance for name-calling, degradation, or any other form of slander against another student. In other words, attack the issue or argument, not the person. A discussion board posting must be 250 words (with a word count noted at the end of each posting) in order to qualify for full points. Each additional posting will earn you 3 points extra credit (up to 15 points extra credit).

The first two postings have been chosen for you. For the first 250-word posting, introduce yourself and tell your classmates something about yourself. What interests you? Why are you in school? What accomplishment are you most proud of? What do you hope to get out of this class (other than an A!)?

In the second posting, elaborate on why you are in this class, in this university, or in your major. How did you arrive at the conclusion to take this course, enroll at UH, or choose your major?

Note: Although there is no "definitive" due date for each discussion board posting, do yourself a favor and keep current with these! The last thing you want to be doing the week of finals is writing thirty-three discussion board postings. And as an added incentive for keeping current, I award 10 points extra credit at the end of the semester if you have kept current.

Summary-Responses: 45 points (4.5%)

Effective summarizing of articles, papers, and books (among other things) is important for writing good research papers. You will be required to write nine summary-responses to *Worlds of Exile and Illusion* by Ursula K. LeGuin. From the following reading schedule, you will need to choose nine sections to write a 500-word summary-response. The first 250 words should be a brief summary of the section you have read. The second 250 words should be your response to the section or the story itself. Consider the following questions when responding (however, you are not limited to these questions):

- Did you like or dislike this section? Why? What was appealing? What made you dislike the story? (Consider setting, character, plot, or other literary elements.) Would you recommend this story?
- What message (implicit or explicit) do you think the author is trying to offer about the present or the future?
- What character did you connect with the most? The least? Why did you make such a connection?
- Can you see parallels between today's society and society of the future?

Due Date: There is no specific due date for these postings; however, like the discussion board postings, you will want to keep current with the suggested due dates (noted in the chart) to ensure that you are not scrambling the week of finals to get these summary-responses in and, more important, that you are prepared to write the final major assignment: the argument paper. Should you choose to write additional postings, you will earn extra credit points (5 points per posting). Please be sure to post under the appropriate heading!

Posting due dates

Page	Due Date
3–28	January 20
28–57	January 27
57–82	February 3
83–115	February 10
115–139	February 17
139–166	February 24
166–190	March 2
190–215	March 9
215–247	March 16
248–276	March 23
276–307	April 6
307–338	April 13
339–370 (end)	April 20

Jill Dahlman, University of Hawaii at Manoa College of Languages, Linguistics, and Literature

Integrating Sources Quizzes (2): 70 points (7%)

Two online, do-at-home, open-book quizzes covering sources, plagiarism, MLA in-text citations, integration of sources, and MLA works cited and APA references lists will be covered. To successfully complete these quizzes, you will need to review these sections in *A Pocket Style Manual*. You may take each quiz *once* at any time *before February 28, 2012*. After February 28, the quizzes will no longer be available, and you will have lost 70 points.

Attendance: 50 points (5%)

In-class assignments are required. Time will be provided to work on these assignments. It is very difficult to work on in-class assignments if you are not in class. Please make every effort to be present in class. Points will be added for each class attended with participation. If you fall asleep, you will lose points. If you are habitually late or leave habitually early, your points will reflect this. If you are text messaging, disruptive, or otherwise not acting as a fully functioning member of this class at any time or in any way violate the University of Hawaii Student Conduct Code, you may be asked to leave, and you will incur an unexcused absence for each occurrence.

Unless you are able to provide written documentation as to why you were not in class (an excused absence, such as a doctor's/employer's note), your absence will be considered unexcused. Four unexcused absences will result in a one-letter reduction in your grade. Please note that if you are not in class for a scheduled peer review, it will be considered a double unexcused absence. Each additional absence (over three) will cost you 10 points. *If you miss six or more classes, you will fail the class—no matter how good your scores are.*

Tardiness in any way, shape, or form is not tolerated. You are expected to be at your job on time. This is your job. Your job is to be in the classroom before the start of class. **Being tardy two times will be considered an unexcused absence.** Because this class uses discussion as one of its methods of teaching, you cannot expect to learn something unless you are sitting in the classroom discussing the material. You are responsible for all missed assignments. And as an added incentive for perfect attendance, I award 10 points extra credit at the end of the semester if you have no absences—excused or unexcused.

Writing Assignments: 270 points (27%)

Assignments are described below. Four major assignments are required. You will determine the remainder of your points for each unit. Drafts and peer reviews are mandatory and are worth points. Without these drafts and peer reviews, you will lose 10% of your grade on each assignment. If you do not attend a peer review session, you will be docked two unexcused absences. Be present at these peer reviews!

Good writing takes time and multiple revisions. The schedule provides you with an opportunity to hand in a draft early in the process, so you will be able to easily complete the assignment. Not only does this method help you understand the process it takes to turn in a good paper, but it also provides you with ample time to complete and revise the assignment. All papers and all drafts must be turned in through the Writing Tab found on CompClass. Each draft that you are turning in for a grade must be submitted through the Writing Tab under the appropriate heading. If, for whatever reason, you cannot upload your document by the due date and time, e-mail the paper to me that night and turn in the paper copy at the beginning of the next regularly scheduled class meeting. If it isn't there before the class starts, it is late and definitely not eligible for full points.

The paper is due on the date indicated. Unless you are dead or in a documented coma, there will be NO EXCEPTIONS. Papers more than two class meeting days late are not eligible for points.

Jill Dahlman, University of Hawaii at Manoa College of Languages, Linguistics, and Literature

BASIC GUIDELINES FOR WRITTEN ASSIGNMENTS

If you follow all of these guidelines, you will earn 2 points extra credit on each major paper and 1 point extra credit on each minor or optional assignment. If you don't follow instructions, you will be docked points as noted.

> Surname, First Name
> English 100/Dahlman
> Topic of/Title of Assignment
> Due Date: Day Year Month

Place your name in the <u>top left corner</u> of the first page as noted.

1. Highlight your thesis (worth 4 points on the major paper/1 point on the minor/option paper) in one color.

2. Highlight each in-text citation in another color (worth 2 points on the major paper/1 point on the minor/option paper).

3. Place a word count at the end of the document (worth 4 points on the major paper/1 point on the minor/option paper).

4. For major papers only: Post your own paper and read postings from the members of this class on Comment.

5. **A bibliography or works cited page** must be attached to each paper (if not attached, a 4-point deduction on the major paper/1-point deduction on the minor/option paper will occur).

6. If you want to know what grade you would have received on any paper, attach a copy of the "general rubric" found at the end of this syllabus. You can print these out from the syllabus that has been posted on CompClass.

7. OPTIONAL (worth 5 points extra credit): Post constructive comments to someone's paper (not necessarily in your peer review group) during the week of peer review (up to two days before the due date). Comments should include the following: a general statement of your impressions after your first quick reading; a specific statement covering what you particularly like and what you see as problematic; and finally, a question that you feel will help the writer in his or her writing process.

8. **Reminder:** ALL FINAL PAPERS ARE DUE ON THE DATE INDICATED—NO EXCEPTIONS!

LEARNING RESOURCES

Students are expected to obtain and bring with them to each class meeting their Working Folder for portfolio workshops (announced and unannounced) and the following books: *A Pocket Style Manual* by Diana Hacker and Nancy Sommers and *Portfolio Keeping*, 2nd Edition, by Nedra Reynolds and Rich Rice. Additionally, students will be required to have an active hawaii.edu account in order to complete the Library Resource Unit and an Internet account to gain access to the discussion board on CompClass. Although you are not required to own a computer, access to both a computer and the Internet is a "must" for this class.

ADDITIONAL INFORMATION

A "University Performance" Standard: Students are expected to make a serious academic commitment to their success in this course. You must at least keep up with the syllabus schedule. Whenever possible, however, it is a good idea to work slightly ahead of the syllabus to compensate for the unexpected.

Jill Dahlman, University of Hawaii at Manoa College of Languages, Linguistics, and Literature

Plagiarism Policy: The University of Hawaii system defines plagiarism as follows:

> Plagiarism includes, but is not limited to, submitting, to satisfy an academic requirement, any document that has been copied in whole or in part from another individual's work without identifying that individual; neglecting to identify as a quotation a documented idea that has not been assimilated into the student's language and style; paraphrasing a passage so closely that the reader is misled as to the source; <u>submitting the same written or oral material in more than one course without obtaining authorization from the instructors involved</u>; and "dry-labbing," which includes obtaining and using experimental data from other students without the express consent of the instructor, utilizing experimental data and laboratory write-ups from other sections of the course or from previous terms, and fabricating data to fit the expected results (emphasis mine).

If you are caught plagiarizing in any manner that even remotely resembles the UH-system policy, you will be dealt with severely. This could include punishment ranging from a zero on the assignment to expulsion from the class or university. If plagiarism is suspected, the student will be expected to conference with me, to produce every single piece of documentation used in the assignment, and to orally defend his or her paper. If concern is still raised, or if the student requests independent assessment, the student shall be expected to appear before a panel of three professors with all evidence of documented sources and to orally defend his or her paper. In short, don't do it.

Incomplete: An Incomplete is not automatically given. An Incomplete is considered only when less than 10% of all coursework is left to complete and only under extreme circumstances. In short, don't expect it.

Grading

A = 900–1,000 points

B = 800–899 points

C = 700–799 points

D = 600–699 points

F = 599 or below

Drop Dates

January 13, 2012 – No record; 100% refund

January 30, 2012 – No record; 50% refund

March 19, 2012 – Drop with a W on your record. Please note: It is far better to receive a W and repeat the course than to receive a D or an F. If you think that you are not going to pass, talk to me before the drop date.

PROPOSED SCHEDULE (NOTE: THIS IS NOT ETCHED IN STONE!)

Key: *WR = Writing and Revising*   *CTA = From Critical Thinking to Argument*

Date	To Be Covered in Class	Homework
WEEK ONE Tuesday 1/10	• Syllabus and expectations	• Post discussion board (DB) postings: 1. Welcome & Introductions 2. "Learning to Read"

Jill Dahlman, University of Hawaii at Manoa College of Languages, Linguistics, and Literature

Thursday 1/12	• General overview of CompClass • Drop date 1/13 with no record and 100% refund	• Post draft of Reflecting paper by midnight Tuesday 1/17 in the Writing Tab • Option paper 1 (Identity) due Tuesday • Read Ch. 1 in *WR*
WEEK TWO Tuesday 1/17	• Draft 1 of Reflecting paper due by midnight • Choose DB topics • Review Ch. 1 in *WR*	• Post DB postings 3 and 4 • Read Ch. 7 in *WR*
Thursday 1/19	• Review Ch. 7 in *WR* • **Option paper 1 (Identity) due**	• Post draft 2 of Reflecting paper in the Writing Tab by midnight Tuesday 1/24 for peer review on Thursday • Complete Summary-Response 1 by Friday 1/20
WEEK THREE Tuesday 1/24	• Peer review of draft 2 of Reflecting paper (due by 1/29) • LIBRARY FIELD TRIP: Class held in Hamilton 113 with Ross Christensen (Head toward the back!)	• Post DB postings 5 and 6 • Option paper 2 (Identity) due Tuesday • Read Ch. 5 in *WR*
Thursday 1/26	• **Option paper 2 (Identity) due** • Choose DB topics • Review Ch. 5 in *WR* • Drop date 1/30 with no record	• Turn in final Reflecting paper and ALL IDENTITY ASSIGNMENTS on Tuesday • Bring in lyrics to song • Complete Summary-Response 2 by Friday 1/27
WEEK FOUR Tuesday 1/31	• **Final Reflecting paper due** • **All Identity Unit assignments due** • Choose DB topics • Rhetoric of music	• Post DB postings 7 and 8 • Read Ch. 5 in *CTA*
Thursday 2/2	• Research proposal due • Rhetoric of music • Review Ch. 5 in *CTA*	• Complete Summary-Response 3 by Friday 2/3 • Option paper 1 (Music) due Tuesday • Post draft 1 of Analysis paper in Writing Tab by midnight on Tuesday • Read Ch. 3 in *CTA*
WEEK FIVE Tuesday 2/7	• Draft 1 of Analysis paper due by midnight • Choose DB topics • Review Ch. 3 in *CTA*	• Post DB postings 9 and 10 • Complete Summary-Response 4 by Friday 2/10 • Read Ch. 4 in *WR*

Jill Dahlman, University of Hawaii at Manoa College of Languages, Linguistics, and Literature

Thursday 2/9	• **Option paper 1 (Music) due** • Review Ch. 4 in *WR*	• Turn in Option paper 2 (Music) on Tuesday • Post draft 2 of Analysis paper in the Writing Tab by midnight on Monday for peer review on Tuesday • Read Ch. 2 in *WR*

WEEK SIX Tuesday 2/14	• Peer review of draft 2 of Analysis paper (due by 2/19) • Choose DB topics • Review Ch. 2 in *WR*	• Post DB postings 11 and 12
Thursday 2/16	• **Option paper 2 (Music) due** • Watch *Star Trek*	• Complete Summary-Response 5 by Friday 2/17 • Turn in final Analysis paper on Tuesday • **All assignments (Music) due Tuesday**

WEEK SEVEN Tuesday 2/21	• **Final Analysis paper due** • **All Music Unit assignments due** • Choose DB topics • Watch *Star Trek: The Next Generation*	• Post DB postings 13 and 14
Thursday 2/23	• Watch *How William Shatner Changed the World*	• Option paper 1 (*Star Trek*) due Tuesday in class • Complete Summary-Response 6 by Friday 2/24 • Post draft 1 of Explaining paper in the Writing Tab by midnight on Tuesday • Read Ch. 11 in *WR*

WEEK EIGHT Tuesday 2/28	• Draft 1 of Explaining paper due by midnight • Choose DB topics • Discussion of annotations • Review Ch. 11 in *WR*	• Annotated Bibliography 1 due Thursday • Read Ch. 2 in *CTA*
Thursday 3/1	• **Option paper 1 (*Star Trek*) due** • Annotated Bibliography 1 due • Review Ch. 2 in *CTA*	• Post DB postings 15 and 16 • Option paper 2 (*Star Trek*) due Tuesday in class • Annotated Bibliography 2 due Tuesday • Complete Summary-Response 7 by Friday 3/2 • Post draft 2 of Explaining paper in the Writing Tab by Monday at midnight for peer review on Tuesday

Jill Dahlman, University of Hawaii at Manoa College of Languages, Linguistics, and Literature

WEEK NINE Tuesday 3/6	• **Class ONLINE!** • Peer review of Explaining paper (due by 3/11) • Annotated Bibliography 2 due	• Complete Summary-Response 8 by Friday 3/9 • Annotated Bibliography 3 due Thursday
Thursday 3/8	• **Class ONLINE!** • **Option paper 2 (*Star Trek*) due** • Annotated Bibliography 3 due	• Post DB postings 17 and 18 • Turn in final Explaining paper on Tuesday • **All Option papers (*Star Trek*) due Tuesday** • Read Ch. 7 in *CTA*

WEEK TEN Tuesday 3/13	• **Final Explaining paper due** • **All *Star Trek* Unit assignments due** • Choose DB topics • Review Ch. 7 in *CTA* • MLA Workshop	• Complete Summary-Response 9 by Friday 3/16 • Annotated Bibliography 4 due Thursday • Read Ch. 4 in *CTA*
Thursday 3/15	• Annotated Bibliography 4 due • Discussion of comic books (in general) • Review Ch. 4 in *CTA*	• Post DB postings 19 and 20 • Option paper 1 (Comics) due Tuesday 3/20 • Annotated Bibliography 5 due Tuesday 3/20 • **Mandatory! Integrating Sources Quizzes (2) due Thursday 3/22**

WEEK ELEVEN Tuesday 3/20	• Annotated Bibliography 5 due • **Option paper 1 (Comics) due** • Choose DB topics	• Post DB postings 21 and 22 • Read Ch. 3 in *WR*
Thursday 3/22	• **Integrating Sources Quizzes (2) due TODAY** • Review Ch. 3 in *WR* • Portfolio/Research Paper Workshop	• Option paper 2 (Comics) due Tuesday • **All Comics papers due Tuesday 4/3** • Read Ch. 1 in *CTA*

WEEK TWELVE Tuesday 3/27	• No school: Spring break • Final drop date 3/19 with no record	
Thursday 3/29	• No school: Spring break	

| WEEK THIRTEEN
Tuesday
4/3 | • **Option paper 2 (Comics) due**
• **All Comics papers due TODAY**
• Choose DB topics
• Review Ch. 1 in *CTA*
• Portfolio/Research Paper Workshop | • Post DB postings 23 and 24
• Rough draft 1 of Argumentation paper due Thursday
• Read Ch. 10 in *WR* |

Thursday 4/5	• **Rough draft 1 of Argumentation paper due** • Review Ch. 10 in *WR* • Portfolio/Research Paper Workshop	• Option paper 1 (SF) due Tuesday • Read Ch. 6 in *CTA*
WEEK FOURTEEN Tuesday 4/10	• **Option paper 1 (SF) due** • Choose DB topics • Review Ch. 6 in *CTA* • Portfolio/Research Paper Workshop	• Post DB posting 25 and 26 • Post draft 2 of Argumentation paper in the Writing Tab by Wednesday at midnight for peer review on Thursday • Read Ch. 6 in *WR*
Thursday 4/12	• **Peer review of Argumentation paper (due by 4/21)** • Review Ch. 6 in *WR* • Portfolio/Research Paper Workshop	• Option paper 2 (SF) due Tuesday • Post draft 1 of Research paper in the Writing Tab by Tuesday at midnight
WEEK FIFTEEN Tuesday 4/17	• Draft 1 of Research paper due by midnight • **Option paper 2 (SF) due** • Choose DB topics • Portfolio/Research Paper Workshop	• Post DB posting 27 and 28 • Final Argumentation paper due Tuesday • **All SF papers due Thursday** • Read Ch. 8 in *WR*
Thursday 4/19	• **Final Argumentation paper due** • **All SF papers due TODAY** • Review Ch. 8 in *WR* • Portfolio/Research Paper Workshop	• Post draft 2 of Research paper in the Writing Tab by Sunday at midnight for peer review on Tuesday • Read Ch. 9 in *WR*
WEEK SIXTEEN Tuesday 4/24	• Draft 2 of Research paper due by midnight • Peer review of Research paper due by 4/30 • Choose DB topics • Review Ch. 9 in *WR* • Presentations!	• Post DB postings 29 and 30
Thursday 4/26	• Presentations!	• Turn in final Research paper and portfolio Tuesday 5/1
WEEK SEVENTEEN Tuesday 5/1	• Presentations! • Portfolio/Research paper due	

Jill Dahlman, University of Hawaii at Manoa College of Languages, Linguistics, and Literature

GENERAL RUBRIC FOR ALL PAPERS
(include with your paper if you want specific feedback)

Item	A–B (✓+)	B–C (✓)	C–D (✓–)
Argument ————	The argument is superior in content.	The argument is average in content.	The argument is below average in content.
Thesis ————	Your thesis is excellent, and your paper follows the thesis.	Your thesis is average, and your paper somewhat follows the thesis.	Your thesis is below average, and your paper does not follow the thesis.
Introduction and conclusion ————	Your introduction and conclusion are on point, and the reader can easily follow your line of reasoning from start to finish.	Your introduction OR conclusion are on point, and the reader can somewhat follow your line of reasoning from start to finish.	Your introduction and conclusion are not on point, and the reader cannot easily follow your line of reasoning from start to finish.
Support ————	Your argument relied on established facts rather than on emotion (no name calling; sticking to the objective facts).	Your argument relied on some established facts rather than on emotion.	Your argument relied heavily on emotion rather than on fact; you often leave your reader wondering what is going on.
Counterargument ————	You took another side into account (acknowledged counterarguments; possibly even refuted a few).	You may not have explicitly taken another side into account, but the viewpoint conveyed in the paper is objective.	You took no other side into account.
Accuracy ————	Your facts were accurate and indicated that you read outside sources for clarity (i.e., you did the homework).	Most of your facts were accurate and indicated that you read some outside sources for clarity (i.e., you did the homework).	Your facts were not accurate and indicated that you had not read outside sources for clarity (i.e., you did not do the homework).
Grammar and punctuation ————	Your grammar and punctuation were excellent, with minimal errors.	Your grammar and punctuation were average, with errors that did not get in the way of the meaning of your paper.	Your grammar and punctuation were below average, with errors that got in the way of the meaning of your paper.
In-text citations ————	Your in-text citations and works cited/bibliography are excellent.	Your in-text citations and works cited/bibliography are average.	Your in-text citations and works cited/bibliography are below average—you need serious help.
Proofreading ————	You have few, if any, corrections to make.	You have a few corrections to make if you want to make this a stellar paper.	You have many corrections to make.

Jill Dahlman, University of Hawaii at Manoa College of Languages, Linguistics, and Literature

Assignment 1: Workshop on Revising Paragraphs

Time required: **20 to 50 minutes**	Pre-workshop homework assignment: Have students bring their handbooks and a copy of their first essay to class.
Purpose: **Teaching paragraph revision**	

Workshop on Revising Paragraphs

As a class, begin by modeling the following steps with a sample paragraph (see handout). Then work individually, in pairs, or in small groups to complete the activity with your own paragraphs. You may want to refer to your handbook's advice on sentence structure, word choice, transitions, topic sentences, and paragraphing. If you are still lost, ask questions!

Activity

1. From your essay, choose a paragraph in need of significant revision, and explain why you think it needs to be revised.

2. Write down the first word or couple of words from each sentence in list form. If you find yourself writing the same words repeatedly, consider other ways you might begin your sentences to create variety. (Later, when you revise your entire essay, you can list the first word for each *paragraph* to check for variety.)

3. Now consider whether your sentences are varied in length. Do your paragraphs contain long sentences or short sentences, or a combination? Use a mix of long and short sentences within each paragraph to avoid monotony and choppiness. Can you combine any sentences? Should some longer sentences be broken into two or more shorter sentences?

4. Consider consistency and coherence. Look back at your thesis sentence and then reread the paragraph you are working on. Is the paragraph clearly related to your thesis? Does it effectively support your main idea? If not, talk with your partner about whether the paragraph is irrelevant and should be removed or whether it can be revised to clearly offer support.

5. In addition to supporting your thesis, each paragraph should focus on one main point. Identify the main ideas in the paragraph. Does the paragraph begin with one point or idea (usually expressed in a topic sentence) and then move on to a new one? If so, you should probably divide those ideas into separate paragraphs. If those new paragraphs are too short or choppy, you may want to add to them, keeping the focus on one main idea.

6. (If you created two paragraphs in step 5, choose only one for discussion in step 6.) Do the sentences in your paragraph proceed smoothly from one idea to the next? For example, if you begin the paragraph with a topic sentence, does your next sentence logically follow and build on that idea? If not, how might you reorganize the paragraph so that each sentence follows logically from the sentence before it?

Laura Detmering, Northern Kentucky University

Assignment 2: Textual Analysis

Time required: At least one week for students to complete a draft outside of class. Allow roughly two weeks for peer review, instructor comments, and revision.	**Purpose:** Teaching textual analysis and argument **Book in use:** *The Arlington Reader*, Second Edition (2008), by Lynn Z. Bloom and Louise Z. Smith

Due dates

Rough draft: Due by e-mail no later than by 5:00 p.m., September 16.
Final draft: Due in class (entire paper packet) on September 30.

Assignment overview

This assignment, an analysis of a text, involves writing similar to what scholars produce for book reviews in academic journals such as *Computers and Composition Online* or *Kairos*. Most published reviews are 1,000 words or less. The norm for publication is 500–800 words, and writing such a brief essay can be a challenge. Writers must decide which details are most important and which insights are pivotal. Luckily for you, this assignment gives you three to five pages to play with so that you have more room to discuss the article in detail. Here's how you start:

- Choose one of the articles below.
- In small groups, summarize key points of the article.
- Think about criteria.
  - Develop specific criteria and apply them to the text. We will brainstorm in class about different criteria and when they are most effectively used. The Source Evaluation Sheet exercise will help with analyzing article content.
- Write your draft. Get feedback. Draft again.
  - Your group's discussion and input will provide a strong foundation, but your essay will be just that—yours. The thesis, argumentative structure, and flow of ideas will be your own.
  - Submit your rough draft as an e-mail attachment. I will return your draft via e-mail with feedback in comment fields.

Articles available in your reader for the textual analysis

- "Notes of a Native Speaker" by Eric Liu; pp. 112–117
- "Blaming the Family for Economic Decline" by Stephanie Coontz; pp. 229–231
- "Every Dictator's Nightmare" by Wole Soyinka; pp. 476–479
- "Designer Genes" by Bill McKibbon; pp. 501–510
- "Life in the Lap of Luxury as Ecosystems Collapse" by William E. Rees; pp. 678–682

Elements of a textual analysis

Your textual analysis should be a fully developed argumentative essay (three pages is okay, but a thorough discussion will likely fill four or five pages) with a clear thesis, an introduction, several body paragraphs, and a conclusion. Before handing it in, check it for the following:

- **A clear introduction to the article:** Be sure that you clearly state the author's name and the article title within the first paragraph of your textual analysis.
- **A brief summary of the article:** Early in your textual analysis, you should include a very brief summary of the article and any background information that the reader might need to understand the topic. Don't assume that the only possible audience is your instructor or that she has already read the article. Your draft will also be read by your peers, who can give valuable feedback on clarity. In addition, your end-of-semester portfolio may be read and evaluated by an instructor who is unfamiliar with these articles. Keep the summary short without sacrificing clarity.

Lanette Cadle, Missouri State University

- **A discussion of the article's audience and purpose:** Whom is the author trying to reach? What information is the author trying to convey to those readers?
- **An evaluation based on relevant criteria:** You must present your own thesis (separate from the author's thesis) regarding the success of the article. Clearly state your overall judgment of the article's effectiveness and note the specific criteria that you have used in making that judgment (for example, validity, quality of research, and attention to important counterarguments).

  To be sure that your criteria are relevant, keep in mind the author's purpose; different audiences have different expectations. For example, it would be unfair to fault the author for using too many technical terms if specialists in the field or even undergraduates in that major are the intended audience. In a case like that, it would be better to simply make a point about the article's value as a research source for undergraduates without relevant scholarly background. You could note that the article uses jargon or assumes background knowledge and recommend that the undergraduate researcher keep a dictionary handy.
- **References and details to support the evaluation:** Assume that your readers do not have the article in front of them or that they have not read it. You need to provide them with specific evidence (in the form of several quotations or paraphrases) to support your conclusions. You also need to explain specifically how this evidence supports your judgment; do not assume that the connection is clear.

  When you quote or paraphrase from the text, include page numbers in parentheses. See your handbook for models.
- **Conclusion:** Offer a fully developed claim about the overall validity of the article. You may remind readers of both good and bad points of the writing. It may be useful to discuss your views concerning the effectiveness of this source for different audiences.

Please feel free to ask me for help, either during office hours (4:30–5:30 Wednesday, before class) or by appointment. I can also answer questions by e-mail. Good luck!

Lanette Cadle, Missouri State University

Assignment 3: Defining and Addressing Plagiarism

Time required: One session of 15 minutes or more for discussion of the assignment. One week is recommended for writing time outside of class.

Purpose: Teaching the meaning of plagiarism and how to avoid it

Resource: This assignment assumes that students are enrolled in CompClass. The assignment can be revised to work without CompClass.

Guidelines

Your goal is to write an in-depth discussion of plagiarism in roughly 1200 words. The key to writing this paper successfully is to choose a focus and support it with evidence. Once you have chosen your focus and done some preliminary research, create an outline. Organize your thoughts as specifically and as logically as possible.

Be sure to define terms that can have multiple or ambiguous meanings so that your reader knows what you mean. Don't assume that your reader agrees with you. As the writer, you guide the reader into a new way of thinking: your own. Be sure you don't lose the reader on the journey!

Finally, remember that a tight thesis will drive your paper (and will make it much easier to write!).

Prompts

The prompts that follow can help you brainstorm. As you think through them, choose just one direction that interests you and will allow you to write a tightly focused essay.

What does plagiarism mean?

- Think back to the first time you heard the word *plagiarism* or participated in a discussion about it. What was the context? What was the message?
- Who owns *your* ideas? What if they've been influenced by outside sources—your parents, school, church, the media?
- How well do you know how to avoid plagiarism? What are your strategies?
- What definitions of plagiarism can you find by doing a Web search? Try the same search in CompClass. What do you discover?
- If you incorporate ideas into your writing after a teacher/tutor conference or peer review, are you plagiarizing?
- A writer's understanding of plagiarism and intellectual property may be culturally defined. In some non-Western cultures, for example, writers might weave the words of others into their own without citation as a gesture of respect and with the understanding that readers recognize the source. Should accommodations be made in American universities for students from such cultures?
- Legal writing and other professional writing often depends on templates and boilerplates. Is this kind of writing plagiarism?
- Remaking movies and songs and repurposing of TV clips are common. Under what circumstances might such activities be considered plagiarism?
- Is there a difference between, say, forgetting to cite something (or not knowing how) and using another person's ideas wholesale without credit? Are both acts plagiarism?
- When people buy things, they assume ownership. When students purchase essays online, do they own those ideas? Should they be able to turn in purchased essays as their own work?

How should we deal with plagiarism?

- What do we call people who have been accused of plagiarism? What do these labels reveal about how we view these people?

→

Jill Dahlman, University of Hawaii at Manoa

- Punishments for academic plagiarism vary widely; look at a sampling of college handbooks (many are online). Should plagiarism punishments be standardized?
- If a first-year student has no prior knowledge of plagiarism, no knowledge of how or why to cite sources, how should the university deal with that person as a writer? Should there be some sort of entry test? A mandatory tutorial? Or a learn-as-you-go policy?

Jill Dahlman, University of Hawaii at Manoa

Time required: One session of at least 50 minutes	**Book in use:** This assignment has been planned with *The Bedford Handbook*, Eighth Edition. It can easily be revised to work with *Rules for Writers* or *A Writer's Reference with Exercises*. Hacker handbooks without built-in exercises can draw on PDF exercises on their book's companion site.
Purpose: Teaching comma usage, run-on sentences, pronoun-antecedent agreement, pronoun reference	
	Preparation: Groups will need to be prepared to share their exercise answers with the class. They can provide handouts or project their work.

Instructions

Using *The Bedford Handbook* (*BH*) as a reference, each group should prepare a ten-minute presentation on the major rules and key terms governing one of the grammatical discussions below. Group members should complete the exercise associated with their topic ahead of time and share their corrections with the class, explaining the reason for each correction or why an already correct item needs no change.

- Each member of the group should take part in the group presentation.
- In addition to preparing their group presentations, students should complete each of the following exercises on their own. Students should raise questions about any exercise items they do not understand during the group presentation on that exercise.

Group 1: Major Uses of the Comma, *BH*, Section 32, Exercise 32–1
Group 2: Unnecessary Commas, *BH*, Section 33, Exercise 33–1
Group 3: Run-on Sentences, *BH*, Section 20, Exercise 20–2
Group 4: Pronoun-Antecedent Agreement, *BH*, Section 22, Exercise 22–1
Group 5: Pronoun Reference, *BH*, Section 23, Exercise 23–1

Bobbie Kilbane, Volunteer State University

Assignment 5: Visual Literacy and Analysis

Time required: Two sessions of at least 50 minutes for prewriting and peer review. Time for writing outside of class.	Preparation: Students should bring a draft and their handbooks for the peer review workshop.
Purpose: Teaching visual analysis	

Task overview

Drawing from the ideas generated in our class discussion, write a two-page essay that analyzes the visual text shared in class. Avoid simply describing the image. Instead, assert a position on the meaning of the image, and show your readers how the elements in the image contribute to the overall meaning of the text.

Purpose of the assignment

- To practice rhetorical analysis through writing about a visual image
- To enhance visual literacy skills
- To practice essay-writing skills

Assignment steps and due dates

1. Prewriting/idea generation: Complete in class on _____.

2. Preliminary draft for peer review workshop: DUE at the beginning of class on _____.

3. Revised drafts: Once you have received feedback from the peer review workshop, revise your draft at least once before you turn it in. I recommend that you complete at least three drafts, taking your second draft to the writing center/lab for additional feedback.

4. **Final draft: DUE on _____.**

Essay guidelines

1. **Introductory paragraph:** Your introduction should (1) engage the reader, (2) provide appropriate background information about the visual text (a brief description), and (3) assert your thesis. In this case, your thesis will be your assertion of what the intended meaning of the image is: What is the image trying to "say" to its audience?

2. **Body paragraphs (at least 3):** Each body paragraph should include a topic sentence that clearly supports the thesis. Each paragraph should (1) identify an element of the visual text that contributes to its overall meaning, (2) briefly describe the element to establish a context for your readers, and (3) explain HOW the element conveys or contributes to the central meaning of the visual text. **Answering the "HOW" part is crucial to your analysis. It is not enough to just identify the characteristics; you must also discuss how these characteristics create meaning or make a statement.**

3. **Concluding paragraph:** The concluding paragraph should (1) evaluate the effectiveness of the visual image and (2) lead the reader out of the essay.

Formatting instructions

Use MLA style for formatting your paper and citing your source (in a works cited page).

Elizabeth Canfield, Virginia Commonwealth University

Assessment guidelines

Successful papers will display the following characteristics:

- A thesis that clearly and fluidly asserts the meaning of the visual text
- Developed body paragraphs that identify, explain, and analyze the elements of the image that contribute to the visual text's overall meaning
- Organization that supports the thesis and helps readers follow your discussion
- Clear, error-free sentences in academic English
- Accurate page formatting and citations in MLA style

Extra help

If you have any specific questions about your draft, stop by my office during office hours or visit the writing center in _____.

Elizabeth Canfield, Virginia Commonwealth University

Assignment 6: Essay 4: Writing in Your Discipline

Time required: Time for writing outside of class. One session of 30 to 50 minutes for group workshops.

Purpose: Teaching writing in the disciplines

Book in use: This assignment works best when students are using *A Writer's Reference with Writing in the Disciplines* or *Writing in the Disciplines: Advice and Models*, a Hacker Handbooks Supplement.

Preparation: Students should bring their Hacker handbook to each class session.

Discipline-specific content: 250 words

Discipline discourse analysis: 500 words

Outline due _____ for group workshops

Rough draft of 500 words for conferences due by beginning of class on _____

Assignment overview

As I stated on the first day of class, ENGL 1101 is not just an English course. It is a writing course administered by specialists in the English department. ENGL 1101 and 1102 are required in part because they prepare you to write for courses in your major. We establish principles such as assignment analysis, coherence, structure, development, and critical thinking. Once you can demonstrate proficiency in these areas, you should be able to transfer those skills to writing assignments in your history, science, philosophy, business, education, and other courses.

This assignment, Essay 4, asks you to create *discipline-specific content* (DSC)—in other words, a short piece of writing in your discipline. Find your major on the following list and see the type of assignment you should produce for the DSC. If your major is not represented on the list, or you have not declared a major, please e-mail me right away! (Note: If you choose an assignment that is NOT associated with any major in the following list, please contact me for approval of your assignment topic.)

DSC assignments by major

1. Business (includes Management, Finance, Marketing)
    You are managing a project for a major insurance company. Insurance premiums are going up across the board at the start of the next calendar year, and you oversee a group of insurance agents who must be informed of the new premiums for different policies. Generally speaking, the major medical policies will increase an average of 25 percent; the dental policies will increase an average of 15 percent; and the eye-care policies will increase an average of 30 percent. Patients covered by policies affected by these premium increases may alter their coverage (number of dependents registered under an account, type of policy, breadth of coverage) during the next open enrollment period, depending on whether they have private coverage or are enrolled under a group plan. Write a memo to the insurance agents you oversee to (a) inform them of the premium increase and (b) explain their role as insurance agents during this transition to higher premiums. Refer to your Hacker handbook for tips on writing well for a business audience.

2. Education (includes Exercise Science, Early Childhood)
    During your time at this university, you will be required to design curricula (plural of *curriculum*) for classes you might teach. Your assignment is to create a lesson plan around the theme of sharing. The concept of sharing is often emphasized as we prepare K–12 students to become part of a larger community. How will your role as a physical education teacher (Exercise Science majors) or an elementary school teacher (Early Childhood majors) dictate how you should teach your students about sharing? Be creative, and refer to your Hacker handbook for the components involved in writing a lesson plan for an audience of educators.

Molly Wright, Columbus State University

3. Art (includes Art History and other related fields)

Whether you are an artist who creates or an art historian, you need a critical framework, a set of ideas about what art is and what makes good art. This critical framework helps you appreciate art on a higher level, and the framework also helps you explain art to others. The best way to develop a critical framework is by learning about various critical theories and practicing your skills by criticizing art. Your assignment is to choose a piece of artwork and critique it. (Provide either a picture of the artwork in the text or a URL where I can look at it online.) Begin by explaining in general terms your framework; feel free to refer to an existing critical school. Then analyze the artwork using that framework, making sure to provide detailed evidence from the work itself. I have made a photocopy from a guide to writing about art that you will receive in class.

4. Sciences (includes Biology, Chemistry, Communication, Pre-Engineering, Nursing, Psychology, Sociology, Computer Science)

When taking science courses related to your major, you will have to know how to write a literature review. These short assignments, which consider and evaluate the findings of a number of research papers, allow students to show that they comprehend the prevailing research. Review an article that I have given you (you will receive it in class unless you request an electronic copy in advance), OR choose an article of your own with my approval. Use the description set forth in your Hacker handbook to guide you as you compose your review.

5. Theater (includes Theater Education)

When exploring the world of theater, you will need to know how to critically assess a performance of a play. Write a review of the film *A Midsummer Night's Dream* (DVD number 3 in the library), analyzing how well the play has been adapted to the screen and discussing the acting, scenery, cinematography, and so on. For a model, see Roger Ebert's review of the film (http://rogerebert .suntimes.com/apps/pbcs.dll/article?AID=/19990514/REVIEWS/905140304/1023).

Discipline discourse analysis

After composing the discipline-specific content of 250 words, write a 500-word analysis of the discussion (or discourse) going on in your field.

Address the following questions:
- What are people writing about in your discipline, and how are they writing about it?
- What are the most common genres of writing in your field (for example, research articles, case studies, lab reports, reviews of literature, critical analyses)?
- How is ENGL 1101 preparing you to write in your discipline?
- What aspects of your writing process should you focus on now, while you are learning the basics, so that you can best prepare yourself for your major courses?

You will be graded on the following:

1. Fulfilling the prompt. (If you need clarification of these instructions, e-mail me or come talk to me about a draft.)

2. A coherent and well-placed thesis/main idea.

3. Using sound, well-developed evidence.

4. Other items as listed on the First-Year Composition rubric.

If you have any questions regarding this assignment, let me know by e-mail or in class.

Molly Wright, Columbus State University